John Calvin Magee

Apostolic Organism

John Calvin Magee
Apostolic Organism
ISBN/EAN: 9783337405359
Printed in Europe, USA, Canada, Australia, Japan
Cover: Foto ©Lupo / pixelio.de

More available books at **www.hansebooks.com**

Apostolic Organism.

BY

J. C. Magee, D. D.

WITH AN INTRODUCTION

BY

J. C. W Coxe, Ph. D., D. D.

CINCINNATI:
CRANSTON & STOWE.
NEW YORK:
HUNT & EATON.
1890.

To
THE YOUNG PEOPLE
OF
Our Pastoral Care.

PREFATORY.

IN what does true visible Churchhood consist? And what is the apostolic pattern for the same, as learned from the facts of history and the precedents and principles of the New Testament? Questions, these, as old as the centuries, and yet as new as the living interest in the same by each succeeding generation. To the consideration of these inquiries is Part I of this essay devoted, while an application of the principles ascertained occupies Part II.

The essayist may be permitted to avow that he has not written with any ambition whatever for authorship, but that these pages have *grown* upon his hands, prompted by a felt need in pastoral work. Hence, those have not been kept in mind who have in their professional libraries the necessary data, and who have the time, the opportunity, and the pressure of professional motive for extended investigation; but with those of our young people and others in mind who may have not such, and to whom a consecutive statement of the topics presented and their consideration as a whole may be a desideratum.

Anything like a polemic spirit is disclaimed, for we "seek peace and pursue it;" the aim has been simply, as pertaining to the matter in hand, to "give a reason for the hope that is in us, with meekness and fear."

From the very nature of the task undertaken, very many sources of information have been drawn upon, and a large number of authorities consulted. This, together with the fact that all the work done has been during such fragments of time as could be spared from ministerial duties, will account for any unevenness of style which may appear. Honest effort has been made, as far as possible, to give credit, duly and fairly, to others, and to cite authorities accurately.

The presumption that any will think the subject sufficiently engaging to read this discussion, can find its apology only in the importance of the issues involved, and their vital relations to steadfastness in Christian and Church life—the thought of any that the subject is of no special interest nor appreciable utility, to the contrary, notwithstanding.

The Holy Scriptures liken the body of believers to a structure, with organs capable of a special function that is essential to the life or well-being of the whole; the Church of the Lord Jesus Christ is, therefore, herein called an *organism*. As the Churches founded personally by the apostles were called Apostolic, so now a body of believers, who are ruled by the doctrines, institutions, practices, etc., found in the Apostolic or New Testament writings, is Apostolic. Therefore consider we APOSTOLIC ORGANISM.

J. C. MAGEE.

MARSHALLTOWN, IOWA, MARCH, 1890.

CONTENTS.

	PAGE.
PREFATORY,	5
INTRODUCTION,	9

PART I.

ALTERNATIVE DOCTRINES OF GENESIS AND ORDER OF A NEW TESTAMENT CHURCH AND OF MINISTERIAL AUTHORIZATION STATED AND EXAMINED.

PRELIMINARY, GOVERNMENT, FACT, FORM, TENDENCY,	15
DOCTRINES STATED,	21
DOCTRINES EXAMINED,	22

CHAPTER I.

TRANSMISSION OR SUCCESSIONISM, ... 23

SECTION   I. Western, Latin, or Roman Catholic Church, ... 26
"   II. Eastern, or Greek Church, ... 65
"   III. Anglican, or Established Church of England 66
"   IV. Anglo-American, or Protestant Episcopal Church, ... 84
"   V. Unitas Fratrum, United Brethren, or Moravian Church, ... 86
"   VI. Culdee Church, ... 89
"   VII. Other Claimants, ... 90
"   VIII. Various Objections Stated, ... 90

CHAPTER II.

DERIVATION, OR ACCREDITIZATION, ... 116

SECTION   I. Church Defined, ... 116
"   II. Ministry, How Scripturally Constituted 138
"   III. Orders and Offices, ... 150
"   IV. Ministerial Prerogatives or Functions, 165

PART II.

HARMONY OF METHODIST EPISCOPAL GENESIS AND ORDER WITH THE PRECEDENTS AND PRINCIPLES OF THE NEW TESTAMENT.

CHAPTER I.

PAGE.

DEVELOPMENT AND FORMATION OF THE METHODIST EPISCOPAL CHURCH, ... 179

SECTION I. Organic Act and Principles, ... 183
" II. Relation of John Wesley to the Organic Act, ... 199
" III. Harmony of Methodist Episcopal Structure with New Testament Uses of the word Church, ... 216
" IV. Ministry—Orders, Offices, Prerogatives 218
" V. Combination of Qualities of Various Forms, ... 230
" VI. Some Methods — Itinerancy, Episcopacy, Presiding Eldership, Class-meetings, Love-feasts, Modes of Worship, Probationary Membership 238
" VII. Duty of All Christians to Sustain Ecclesiastical Order, ... 254
" VIII. Conclusion, ... 257

INTRODUCTION.

A NEW book demands a *raison d'être*. Why this book? The answer is not far to seek. "Apostolic Organism" is not a work of supererogation. It is not a Quixotic assault upon a wind-mill. In it will be found no knight-errantry. The author has no call to assail or withstand dead foes. He is himself too thoroughly alive to be satisfied with a moribund cause. He is intent on peace; hence his choice of keenest weapons and of most advantageous positions. He does not defend his fortress by marching out his garrison. Conquest does not mean surrender. Thorough self-respect asks only for a fair field and no concessions. Cowardice never produces conviction. A rational faith calls for no compromise. Apologetics are not here in order. A challenge of one's right to be, invites candid questioning as to what life is. This the author has undertaken. The issue discussed is both old and new. The matter is apostolic; the method is modern; the spirit is irenic. To determine "the signs of an apostle" is the aim; to determine the legitimacy of Succession as well. The work, though brief, is well done; the merit of this *brochure* is neither scant nor obscure. It is written in an attractive style; the argument is conducted in a candid and judicial spirit, as free from bigotry as it is from cant; the historical data adduced are ample and valid; and the conclusions reached abundantly vindicate the apostolicity of our Church organism, without, on the one hand, making the baseless claim of exclusive tactual succession, or conceding, on the other, the futility of any attempt to identify the Church of to-day with that of the apostolic period. The author has written from the stand-point of a pastor, with a distinct perception of the needs of the people. I am confident that his work will prove a boon to the younger members of the Methodist Episcopal Church, while it will be read with pleasure and profit by mature minds both in the ministry and laity.

J. C. W. COXE.

Part One.

ALTERNATIVE DOCTRINES OF GENESIS AND ORDER OF A NEW TESTAMENT CHURCH AND OF MINISTERIAL AUTHORIZATION STATED AND EXAMINED.

Apostolic Organism.

PRELIMINARY.

GOVERNMENT, FACT, FORM, TENDENCY.

GREAT facts have great underlying philosophic principles; and great institutions, not only reasons why they exist, but rational methods by which they came into and continue in existence. There is a philosophy of history, as well as a history of philosophy. "History," it is declared, "is philosophy teaching by example."

Because of the varied relations of man, government has been one of the world's great facts. In both civil and ecclesiastical affairs, order and stability have always been a desideratum.

In civil fabrics three principal forms of government have obtained, all others being but modifications or combinations of these; namely, Monarchy, Aristocracy, Democracy. The first, being executed by the authority of a single individual, the throne of power being obtained by hereditary descent and held through life, when absolute or autocratic, the executive rules without ministry, parliament, or council; when despotic, he governs by his own will, with oppression, and without established law; when limited, the power is restrained by a constitution and a representative assembly of the people governed.

In the second the nobles of a country govern conjointly—an oligarchy, being nearly allied to it, obtaining where a few, either nobles or plebeians, rule ;t his form usually arises where, in the revolution of empires, the former ruler is deposed.

In the third, power is lodged wholly in the hands of the people collectively. A republic is the same principle, only administered by representatives chosen by the people.

Anarchy is a want of government, a state of lawless confusion, being, of all conditions, the very worst possible, even tyranny being preferable—the worst government being better than none at all.

The tendency of each form, because of human selfishness, is to an accumulation of power,—in the first, to become more and more despotic; in the second, the officers of government incline to act for their own personal interests, as against the good of the people; in the third, government inclines to become more and more liberal, and, if unrestrained and unsustained by the highest order of patriotism and public virtue, will terminate in anarchy and ruin.

The Church of the living God is the most exalted organism on the face of the earth, it being not a mere society or fraternity, but a fellowship originating in heaven, the place of its glorious destination; it is identified with the very highest interests of humanity in time and in eternity. The absolute necessity of some form of Church government, with plenary power properly vested to receive members, hear complaints, and exclude the incorrigible, is clearly obvious; no society, fraternity, or fellowship, being able to long exist without power to do all things necessary to its well government and preservation (*cf.* Watson's Institues, Part IV, ch. i). Many, impatient of restraint and unwilling to be subject to Church order, have called the New Testament their Discipline, and, conveniently understanding it to suit their feelings, have sought to form and perpetuate Churches without efficient governments; but such have usually proved short-lived, like Jonah's gourd, and the hue and cry of liberty, dying away, serves no purpose but to warn of the folly of such useless efforts.

The principal forms of Church government which have obtained since the introduction of the gospel are, namely, Independent, Congregational, Presbyterian, and Episcopal.

In Independency, all ecclesiastical power originates and remains with the local assembly or

Church, it elevating one of its own number to ministry. In Congregationalism, the same definition obtains, with the additional element of *consociation* with neighboring Churches for purposes of mutual advice and co-operation in matters of discipline, and *association* of ministers of those Churches for the same purposes, and mutual helpfulness. In Presbyterianism, power is quite largely lodged in the Presbytery, consisting wholly of elders, one preaching and one ruling (a layman) from each Church or congregation; and the affairs of the local Church quite largely administered by its life-tenure officiary, constituting a Session for such purpose. In Episcopalianism, two salient views obtain: First. Prelatical Episcopacy, which, in its turn, is maintained by two views,—(a) That ecclesiastical authority has lineally descended from the apostles to the bishops, who are held to be a superior order, holding authority over the inferior clergy, the presbyters or priests, and the deacons, and that the high functions connected with ordination to ministry and general superintendence over ministers and Churches, is the divinely enjoined and inherent prerogative of this class of officers. While the advocates of this view will grant that God has left men at liberty to modify every other kind of government, according to the needs and circumstances, they will yet contend that one form of government for the Church is unalterably fixed by divine appointment, and that theirs is that one, absolutely *essential* to the existence of the Church. (*b*) That the primacy of St. Peter has descended through the line of the bishops of Rome, and that the true Church and true Churchliness can be found only where this descent, with all its hierarchical accompaniments, can be traced.

As the result of this view, there have been unlimited confusion and uncertainty. As applied by Rome, it excludes from Christendom all of the Eastern Churches before the Reformation, and the entire Protestant world since. As applied by Protestant High-Churchism, while untenable on its own grounds, it yet cuts off all other episcopal and all non-episcopal communions, declaring that wherever it is wanting there is no Church, no regular ministry, no valid ordinances; and that all who are united with religious societies not conforming to this order are "aliens from Christ," "out of the appointed way to heaven," and have no hope but in the "uncovenanted mercies of God."

Charity leads us to hope that it is but a small contingent who hold this extravagant view. Indeed, many prelatists hold it with great modification, saying that the government of the Church by bishops, as a superior order to presbyters, was sanctioned by apostolic example, and that it is the duty of all Churches to imitate this example; but, while considering episcopacy as necessary to the highest perfection of the Church, they magnanimously concede that it is by no means necessary to the existence of Church-life; and accordingly acknowledge, as true though incomplete Churches of Christ, many in which the episcopal doctrine is rejected, and other principles made the basis of ecclesiastical government.

Second. Moderate Episcopacy holds that neither Christ nor his apostles prescribed any particular form of ecclesiastical government, to which the Church must positively adhere in all ages and under all circumstances; but that he and they simply indicated general or constitutional principles, leaving their application of details, or statutory enactments to Christian expediency. It agrees with Independency and Congregationalism in maintaining that all ecclesiastical authority, by Divine institution, *originates* in the Body of Believers—the Church—but parts hands with them when they aver that the exercise of such authority must *reside* or *remain* there; holding that the body where authority *originates* may lodge its exercise in a properly constituted executive, under suitable constitutional checks and balances; and, requiring accountableness back to itself, may order such things as are Scripturally and historically allowable for the attainment of the highest ends— a true Church objective—as the needs of the work from time to time demand. This includes supervisory power over pastors and the Church at large, as well as pastoral supervision over particular Churches. Hence, while recognizing the equality of ministerial *order*, it also recognizes diversity in *jurisdiction*. In advocacy of this view there have been many of the most pious and learned of earth.

The tendencies of these forms of Church government, like those of the State, if unrestrained by proper checks and balances, is for power to accrete or accumulate in the direction in which it is lodged.

The tendency of a government which is an amalgam or union of the best phases of all, will be an interesting study in its proper place.

May the Good Spirit guide us into a desire to know the truth as we proceed!

DOCTRINES STATED.

WHAT is the legitimate genesis, beginning, or origination, of a particular Church? Whence are ecclesiastical constitution and order? What the source and method of legal ministerial commission? In reply, there are two sharply defined, and, we may say, rigidly alternative doctrines; namely,—

First. A Church is a divinely constituted

organism, a body of Believers in covenanted compact, providentially associated for the ends and purposes of the Christian life; incumbency in the ministerial office therein originating in the call of God, and *deriving* its legal ecclesiastical status by the accreditization of the Church, acting in the name of the Lord Jesus, the Head of the Church, and the sole source of all authority in his kingdom.

Second. A Church is a corporate body, existing intact in external documentary form from the beginning of the Christian era; ministerial or priestly functions and status therein being *transmitted* in consecutively successive commissions by the authority of the ordainer to the ordained, by the imposition of hands and accompanying ceremonies.

The first we shall call the doctrine of *Derivation*, or accreditization; the second, the doctrine of *Transmission*, or successionism.

DOCTRINES EXAMINED.

Reversing the order, we first consider the doctrine of Transmission, or successionism.

CHAPTER I.

TRANSMISSION, OR SUCCESSIONISM.

AS a fair statement of this doctrine, whether it be held by papists or Protestant High-Churchmen, I quote from a work entitled, "Apostolical Succession in the Church of England," by Arthur W. Haddan, B. D., which is put forth as representative of the standard doctrine on that theme, in which it is said, in chapter i: "The doctrine of Apostolical Succession means that, according to the institution of Christ, a ministry ordained in due form by [episcopal] succession from the apostles, and so from our Lord himself, is an integral part of that visible Church of Christ upon earth to which Christian men are to be joined. It implies, further, that the ministry so ordained is not a merely external office of convenience and of outward government, but involves also the transmission of special gifts of grace, in order to the carrying on in the Church of the supernatural work of Christ by his Spirit. For although, no doubt, it might have been appointed that even a merely outward office of convenient order should have required a supernatural authorization, yet it is more intelligible, and seems more necessary, and is actually part of the doctrines as held by the Church, that a supernatural work should need a supernatural sanction, and that what is rightly held to be the grace of orders, and not a merely outward appointment, should be transmitted by those only who have themselves, in succession, received that grace, and the authority to transmit it, from its own original source."

As items implied in a belief of this statement of an apostolic ministry, the same author proceeds to state, under six heads: "1. A belief in the continued need of supernatural gifts, a supernatural revelation of truth, and a supernatural gift of spiritual life,—a belief in *the grace of God*. 2. That these gifts of grace are intrusted to a corporate body, established and continued in the world by God himself, and that they are to be obtained ordinarily and primarily by the individual Christian, as in union with Christ through this his mystical body upon earth. . . . 3. A belief that in this Church there is a divinely constituted ministry, . . . *an order of clergy*, . . . men to whom God, by his appointed instruments, has intrusted certain authority and powers—a message of truth to be delivered and gifts of grace to be dispensed,—*ministers of the Word and sacraments*. 4. A belief in the *grace of orders;*

i. e., in the necessity and in the spiritual effectiveness of a proper formal ordination. 5. A belief in *episcopal ordination.* 6. Lastly, if the grace of orders be a grace at all, we are brought, in the end, to that which is specially intended by Apostolical Succession, viz., to a belief that the gift of orders, so transmitted by the bishop, with the laying of the hand of the Presbytery, must needs have descended *in unbroken line* from those who first had it, viz., the apostles. All this scheme of doctrine," he continues, "obviously is of one piece, and holds together as one complete and homogeneous view of the way of God's dealings with Christian men. It means, in a few words, without bishops, no presbyters; without bishops and presbyters, no legitimate certainty of sacraments; and without sacraments, no certain union with the mystical body of Christ, viz., with his Church. Without this, no certain union with Christ; and without that union, no salvation."

In a moment of tenderness Mr. Haddan's Christian charity rises superior to his logic, and he says: "It is true, no doubt, that those Christian communities who have no such ministry do, nevertheless, on the one hand, cling to parts of the scheme of doctrine—some more, some less— to which it belongs, and repudiate often, and many of them maintain, extremely opposite views;

and that, on the other, they show proofs in Christian love and earnestness that the grace of God, from the ordinary channels of which they have cut themselves off, has, nevertheless, overflowed its bounds, and reaches over to them." This ebullition of generosity would not find favor with all who advocate the former statements of that author. However, we are thankful to Mr. Haddan for "small favors," and are abundantly capable of being "proportionately so for large ones."

The complexion to which the whole matter must finally come is simply this: Can such a doctrine be sustained Scripturally, historically, morally? To such inquiry we address ourselves, examining patiently every possible link in such a chain.

Section I.

IS THE DOCTRINE OF TRANSMISSION DEMONSTRABLE THROUGH THE WESTERN, OR LATIN, CHURCH, COMMONLY KNOWN AS THE ROMAN CATHOLIC?

The papal claim runs thus: Peter the apostle was given, by our Lord Jesus Christ, a visible headship of the whole militant Church; and a primacy, not of honor and rank alone, but of direct and sovereign jurisdiction over all the other apostles; that this primacy was not limited to Peter's person only for his life-time, but was conferred on him with power to bequeath it to his successors; and that he did so bequeath it to the bishops of Rome, and that it has continued in unbroken descent through the Christian centuries.

This claim for what the modern Roman theologians have called the "Privilege of Peter," as set forth in the first two propositions above, in order to be accounted divine in the Church of Rome, and warranted by Revelation, must be based (a) on Holy Scripture, (b) on the historical tradition of the Church, (c) on the unanimous consent of the fathers. The proof of the third and concluding proposition above, must depend upon the evidence of Church history subsequent to the New Testament period.

The charter or conveyance by which such a right could be given to Peter needs to be very express and clear, because *privilege* being a private exception to the usual public course of law, either in the form of exemption from some burden generally imposed or of enjoyment of some benefit generally withheld, is essentially an invidious thing, and requires fuller proof than any other right before it can be allowed as valid.

An examination of the Holy Scriptures, not from a theological but a legal point of view, is vital to the issue. Our Lord's charter to St. Peter is held to be contained in the three following clauses of the Gospels, namely:

1. "And Jesus answered and said unto him,

Blessed art thou, Simon Bar-jona: for flesh and blood hath not revealed it unto thee, but my Father which is in heaven. And I say also unto thee, That thou art Peter, and upon this rock I will build my church; and the gates of hell shall not prevail against it. And I will give unto thee the keys of the kingdom of heaven; and whatsoever thou shalt bind on earth shall be bound in heaven; and whatsoever thou shalt loose on earth shall be loosed in heaven." (Matt. xvi, 17-19.)

2. "And the Lord said, Simon, Simon, behold, Satan hath desired to have you, that he may sift you as wheat: but I have prayed for thee, that thy faith fail not: and when thou art converted, strengthen thy brethren." (Luke xxii, 31, 32.)

3. "So when they had dined, Jesus said to Simon Peter, Simon, son of Jonas, lovest thou me more than these? He saith unto him, Yea, Lord; thou knowest that I love thee. He saith unto him, Feed my lambs. He saith unto him again the second time, Simon, son of Jonas, lovest thou me? He saith unto him, Yea, Lord; thou knowest that I love thee. He saith unto him, Feed my sheep. He saith unto him the third time, Simon, son of Jonas, lovest thou me? Peter was grieved because he said unto him the third time, Lovest thou me? And he said unto him, Lord,

thou knowest all things; thou knowest that I love thee. Jesus saith unto him, Feed my sheep." (John xxi, 15–17.)

This is the sum total of the charter. In noticing these Scriptures the following facts are apparent: First. By reference to the Greek text of the passage in Matthew, in connection with that of the partially parallel passage in John i, 42, there is unquestionably an ambiguity of wording which is not certain, manifest, and unmistakable in meaning, a peculiarity reproduced by the Vulgate, thus failing to satisfy the condition required by the canonists that the wording must be certain and manifest, not obscure or doubtful. Obviously the words can not be obscure or ambiguous in expressing what the Lord Jesus actually meant; but, in order to warrant the stress laid by Roman theologians, the *same* word should be used in both clauses of the sentence, which is not. As the clauses actually stand, there is contrast as well as likeness implied; and the *stone*, although akin to the *rock*, is something different and apart from, less in dimensions, stability, and importance.

Furthermore, the analogy of faith demands that the Gospel shall always be, at the very least, on an equality with the law, and that, wherever possible, it shall move in a higher plane; but that it shall never descend, under any circumstances whatever, to a lower level, much less substitute a type for a reality, a shadow for a substance. Now, wherever in the Old Testament the word *rock* is spiritually used to denote either the basis and strength of the Hebrew Church, or the refuge and confidence of a single believer, it invariably means none save Almighty God himself, in which sense it occurs very many times—*e. g.*, Deut. xxii, 4; Deut. xxxii, 18; 1 Sam. ii, 2; 2 Sam. xxii, 2, 3, 32; 2 Sam. xxiii, 3; Psa. lxii, 1, 2; Isa. xxvi, 4 (margin); Isa. xliv, 8 (margin), *et al.* The same identity of spiritual application is preserved by our Lord in the New Testament, Matt. vii, 24, 25; Luke vi, 47, 48; and by Paul, 1 Cor. x, 4, and 1 Cor. iii, 2.

Second. The prerogative expressed, whatever it may have been, was not peculiar to Peter, but common to others. Was not the question put to the whole twelve? Did not Peter answer for the whole twelve in the mighty confession which he uttered relative to the God-man? More; we are told that in what appears to be the interval between Peter's going away to pay the tribute-money for Christ and himself (Matt. xvii, 27), and his return to the other apostles, when he put his question to Christ on the forgiveness of injuries, our Lord conferred the same power of binding and loosing on the remaining apostles, apart from Peter, saying: "Verily, I say unto you, Whatsoever ye shall bind on earth shall be bound in heaven" (Matt. xviii, 18); and again bestowed it on all the apostles collectively after his resurrection (John xx, 21-23).

The second passage, that from Luke, so far from exalting Peter, actually puts him below the level of his colleagues, as the context shows. All of them are to be tried, and sifted by Satan like wheat. Peter is the only one whose actual fall and denial of his Lord is foretold—cowardly flight being the worst fault of the other apostles— and thus he is the only one who stands in need of being converted from the apostasy. And he is bidden, when this necessary repentance and change have taken place in himself, to support, by his newly revived zeal, his yet unfallen brethren, lest they should sin as he had just done. To fortify them by confession of his own weakness, is in no respect, I submit, akin to exercising authority over them.

The third passage, that in John, while it is the only place where the apostles are spoken of as "sheep," includes Peter as one of them, and in no way designates him as their shepherd; in like manner it confers no exceptional privilege, because we have it twice attributed to the elders of the Church. (Acts xx, 28; 1 Peter v, 1-3.) In truth, furthermore, part of the immediate context of John xxi, 17, furnishes incidental but adequate disproof of the popish claim. (John xxi, 20-22.) It is obvious that, if Peter had received jurisdiction over John only a few moments before, his question was perfectly legitimate and reasonable, and merited a reply as being his concern, because affecting one for whom he had been just made responsible. But the answer he actually receives can denote nothing short of John's entire independence, and the restriction of Peter's own commission to attending to his own specific and limited share of apostolic work, with no right of control over John.

Therefore it is an inevitable and irresistible conclusion that the interpretation which makes Peter alone personally "the rock" upon which the Church is built, is an *eisegesis*—that is, reading a meaning into it—rather than an *exegesis*, or drawing its own meaning out of it; and that not Peter alone, but each and every apostle was a rock, and a recipient of the keys as well, and all were coequal in powers. Indeed, the Church is expressly said (Eph. ii, 20, doubtless in allusion to the foregoing passages) to be built on the foundation of the prophets and apostles, "Jesus Christ himself being the chief corner-stone"—"apostles," not apostle. All of the apostles were Peters, or stones, of the foundation, as well as he.

Inasmuch as the whole New Testament ought, for the purposes of this inquiry, to be construed as a single document, there are a number of expressions and apparent indications, but a collation of them is impossible herein for want of space.

An investigation of the early Liturgies and comments of the Church Fathers, and the Canons and Decrees of the early Councils,* results, to say the very least, in establishing the charter of the "Privilege of Peter."

The effort to establish the proposition that Peter was constituted primate in the Apostolic Church failing, the proposition of a successional attribute for him goes with it. The only question in this connection to receive consideration is: *Was the apostle Peter ever actually Bishop of Rome?* This is the first link in the chain, not to say the staple by which the chain is attached to the Heavenly Throne. Is it not passing strange that the Holy Scriptures are absolutely and ominously silent on a subject upon which so much has been staked by papal assumptions, except that it contains very strongly adverse presumptive evidence? Not merely is there no positive proof that he was ever Bishop of Rome, or that he ever lived there and exercised the pastoral office, but there are certain statements which are

---

*The student especially interested will do well to investigate "Petrine Claims," by Dr. Littledale.

irreconcilable, on any hypothesis, with the theory that he was, and that he did actually sit as such for twenty-five years, dying there, a martyr by crucifixion, on the very same day—June 29, A. D. 67—as that on which Paul was beheaded. Papists claim, it is true, that Peter came to Rome in the second year of the Emperor Claudius, for the purpose of counteracting the influence of Simon Magus. This second year of Claudius occurred A. D. 43, but from Acts xii, 3, 4, we learn that Peter was a resident at Jerusalem, and was there cast into prison by Herod Agrippa in the last year of his reign (verse 23), which was in the fourth year of Claudius. Thus, two years after the time when Roman Catholic writers affirm that Peter took up his abode in Rome as the bishop of that Church, and was administering there as such, he was in prison at Jerusalem.*

In Acts xv, 6, Peter is spoken of as still at Jerusalem, in the ninth, some say eleventh, year of Claudius. In Acts xxviii, 17, it is recorded that Paul came to Rome, a prisoner, in the seventh year of Nero; that is, A. D. 60 (some say 62, and others, with more probability, even 63), but, on this occasion, not the slightest mention is made of Peter being at Rome. Neither do the

---

* For citation of authorities covering this matter, see "Romanism of Low-Churchism, and End of Prelacy," by R. C. Shimeall, pp. 288-292. Also, "Petrine Claims." by Littledale.

Jews name him, nor do the Christians there, for the gospel had been introduced into Rome very early, possibly by converts of the day of Pentecost (Acts ii, 10, 41), though many came out to meet Paul. When Paul arrived in Rome, he sent for the resident Jews there, who were very glad to meet with an apostle, from whom they could learn distinctly what that new religion was, of which they only knew that it was "everywhere spoken against." (Acts xxviii, 22.) Up to that time, therefore, neither Peter, nor any other apostle, had preached the gospel at Rome. Another strange fact is that in the whole Epistle to the Romans, written A. D. 58, no mention is made of Peter, much less as the resident Bishop of Rome. This is the more remarkable, as in the epistle many persons are referred to by name, with salutations, and as Paul was accustomed to refer to Peter, when addressing Churches which Peter had either founded or to which he was known (*e. g.* 1 Cor. i, 12–15; iii, 22; ix, 5; Gal. i, 18; ii, 7, 8, 9, 14). There is not the slightest evidence, as late as A. D. 63, that Peter had any personal or official connection with the Church at Rome; and if he ever had subsequently, it can not be proven from the New Testament, and must be decided by post-Biblical testimonies.* Church history gives no

---

* See Schaff's History of the Christian Church, Vol. I, page 251.

account of it. Kurtz says (Church History, page 65): "This whole legend about Peter's bishopric at Rome (according to Eusebius, from the year 42 to 67), is derived from the heretical pseudo-epigraphic Clementines and Recognitions—an authority entirely untrustworthy."

Rather a poor beginning, I am bound to say, for a doctrine in which, it is maintained by its adherents, are involved "the spiritual interests of millions."

A doctrine upon which arrogant assumption builds so much, should not be established on conjecture, or on something taken for granted, but should be *demonstrably* certain. In the abstract of title no "cloud" should appear, certainly not in the original patent most of all. But we must conclude that at this point the claim of external successionism is involved in *impenetrable confusion and dark uncertainty.*

The fact is, there are other apostles who might have urged a claim to the primacy superior to that of Peter. Did not *James* preside in the convocation in Jerusalem? (Acts xv.) Was it not *John* of whom Jesus said, "If I will that he tarry till I come," and which was construed to mean, though erroneously, that "he should not die?" Was he not the special friend of Jesus, leaning on his bosom at the Paschal Supper, and did he not receive from the tremulous lips of

Jesus, when hanging quivering on the cross, the tender charge to be a son to Mary, his weeping mother? Did he not long linger as the patriarch of Christianity, and, on Patmos, rapt in the visions of the future, become the amanuensis of the Spirit, in recording the prophetic fortunes of the Church to the close of time? How came it that the *supremacy* was never claimed for him,— the fittest of all to receive it, I may presume to say?

And there is *Paul:* while Peter, singularly enough, is careful not to appropriate the title of *paternity*, in his relation to the Church—for, as if with some prophetic foresight, his words are studiously *fraternal:* "To the elders which are among you, I exhort, who am also an *elder*" (1 Peter v, 1)—yet Paul does employ parental phraseology, for he calls Timothy his own *son* in the faith, and his "dearly beloved son;" and Titus, "his own son after the common faith" (1 Tim. i, 1). So far as the appellation is concerned, Paul, and not Peter, was the first *pope* (papa, father). However, Paul did not use these names in the *official* sense, but as expressive of that paternity which grew out of the spiritual relation to him of those who, "in Christ Jesus, he had *begotten* through the gospel." (1 Cor. iv, 15.) When he speaks of office, he uses the word expressive of the *fraternal* bond: "Paul, an apostle of Jesus Christ, and Timothy, our brother." (Philemon 1.) Additionally, Peter had a *wife* (Matt. viii, 14), and, on the Romish hypothesis of the celibacy of the clergy, it ought to be worthy of note that Paul was a bachelor (1 Cor. vii, 8)! and hence had a better claim to the primacy, if there were one. Again, *did Peter, if he did receive authority to transmit his peculiar privilege, whatever it was, to his successors in office, actually do so?*

Who was the second Bishop of Rome? Here, again, all is confusion. Some of the Fathers say Clement; others, Linus; still others, Cletus. The papist writers themselves admit that the order of the succession is uncertain. As to who may have been *the second, third, and fourth* Bishop of Rome, there is not only confusion, but the most palpable contradictions. Linus, Cletus, and Clement being declared, to be sure, by some; others, that Linus and Cletus were only coadjutors to the apostle Peter.

As to who was the immediate successor of Peter, one popish biographer of the popes, a high authority in his way, claims that Peter, just before his martyrdom and in full view of it, ordained Clement Bishop of Rome, transferring all his powers to him. This, of course, is contradicted by others; besides, according to the dates, it appears that Peter had been dead twenty years when Clement is said to have become bishop, and yet they say Peter made him Bishop of Rome! But I must not forget that this is no difficulty with a miracle-working Church! Twenty years, sooner or later, is a mere circumstance! However, I plainly see that, to those who do not begin with a full and implicit faith in the *dicta* of "the Church," the first four links in the chain are so doubtful as to forbid the placing of any confidence in them whatever.

Second. All the inextricable confusion and uncertainty attending the first step in the so-called succession is, however, a matter of little moment to the Romanist, as his succession is not episcopal, or in a line of bishops, *but in the papal chair*. In the Romish law the three great points are, *Legal Election, Canonical Induction, and Actual Possession of the Chair;* and for centuries the last of these three atoned for any and all faults or flaws in the legal requirements. A pope could make or mend any enactment, or supply any virtue, for any cause, by reason of his supremacy in the Church.

The utter impossibility, however, of tracing transmission by these requirements is manifest by the following considerations:

(*1.*) *The Manner of Electing the Popes.* Methods, such as "intrigue, contention, violence, bribery, and bloodshed," of which the papal historians themselves tell, were common, by which men who were religiously inclined were thrust into the background; whilst those who were determined to secure the papal throne at all hazards and at any expense, became the prominent and successful candidates. The details of the history of these events are immeasurably shocking, and show how "might made right" and arbitrary sway held high carnival. Mosheim says (Vol. II, page 120): "Theodora, a very lewd woman, who controlled all things at Rome, made John X, who was archbishop of Ravenna, succeed to the papal chair. For, at this time, nothing was conducted regularly at Rome, but everything was carried by bribery or violence." The election of Alexander VI, a Spaniard by birth, whose name was Roderic Borgia, is related to have occurred on this wise: After the funeral obsequies of Pope Innocent VIII, the cardinals shut themselves up in the conclave to choose a successor. In order to secure the votes of a majority of the cardinals, he entered into a solemn bargain, that Cardinal Orsino should have a palace and two castles; that Ascanius Sforza should be made vice-chancellor of the Church; that Colonna should have the abbey of St. Benedict, with all the castles and right of patronage, to him and his family forever; that St. Angelo should have the bishopric of Porto, with the town and furniture, and particularly the cellar full of wine. To the cardinal of Parma he gave the city of Nepi. To Savelli he made over the town of Citta-Castellana, with the Church of St. Mary Major. On many others he bestowed many thousand ducats. For one vote, that of a white friar of Venice, he gave five thousand ducats of gold. To one of the cardinals was given, prior to the election, four mules loaded with silver plate. It was thus by simony that a majority was secured, and Roderic Borgia was elected and declared pope by the name of Alexander VI. (Gordon's Life of Alexander VI.) And of the life and actions of this man, it is declared that they show that there was a Nero among the popes as well as among the emperors.

It was no uncommon thing for one pope to excommunicate another, to curse and annul all his acts, including the sacraments. Two popes were put to death. Six were driven out and dethroned by those who aspired to their places. It is a sorry exhibit, we must all confess, of "a holy mother Church." The picture, however, has been drawn by her own faithful children.

It enables us to judge as to the clearness, certainty, and value—or, rather, the obscurity, uncertainty, and worthlessness—of an apostolicity or apostolic succession coming down through channels so filthy and so bloody. No wonder Bishop Stillingfleet (Church of England) should say: "The succession is as muddy as the Tiber itself."

There has, too, been a total want of uniformity in the method of conducting the pontifical elections. The tradition is that Peter *appointed* his successor. Why has not the Church of Rome imitated his example, if this be so? But *seven other modes* have obtained: Nominations by the bishops, but elections by the priests and people; nominations by the emperor or empress on their own responsibility, and election by the bishops; the transfer of the whole power to the emperor by Leo VIII; according to Cardinal Baronius, the popes were introduced by powerful men and women; that it was frequently the price of prostitution. Then, by the decree of the Pope Nicholas II, in his Lateran Synod, the whole business was given over to the cardinals—an order of men not heard of for the first thousand years after Christ! This occurred A. D. 1059. Then came the appointment of the popes by general councils—as those of Pisa, Constance, and Basil. And, finally, back to the plan enacted by Nicholas II, which constitutes the present mode; namely, the popes make cardinals, and cardinals make the pope! And so intermingled are the schemes of the cardinals with the political affairs of the various nations that, on the election of a pope, we hear it said: "Austria has succeeded," or "Spain" or

"France has prevailed this time," or the "Italians are ahead again."

But, possibly, it is said: "What difference does it make how the election is conducted?" Well, presumably, very little difference to practical people, but to the "red-tape sticklers" for having all things in form, as they were, logical consistency compels that they adhere to the original method; and, if the original Peter "appointed" his successors, all imitative Peters must also appoint their successors, and any other method is nothing short of unapostolic. There is a right way, and a wrong way; if to appoint his successor by an incumbent is the right way, all other ways are wrong. He who can be satisfied that there is purity and legitimacy of succession in the heterogeneous manner of the pontifical elections, is welcome to his belief, and to any succession that may come to him through channels so filthy and so bloody.

(*2.*) *The palpable defects in the best authenticated lists, or registers, of the alleged succession, likewise demonstrate the fallacy of the claim.*

This theory of the transmission direct of the grace, office, and functions apostolic, "by the hands of the apostles," absolutely excludes the idea of an intervening space, as to time, in uniting the consecutive links.

That there is the greatest lack of uniformity

and agreement among the chroniclers of the successive links is apparent to any one who will, even though but casually, examine the various tabular genealogical registers which are available. In the Romish line it is essential that the hands of Peter should be employed in forging and welding the links next following, or, rather, the first link which attaches to the staple. Others might assist at the anvil, but to him alone belonged the fire that could fuse, and thus prepare it for and adjust it to its proper fastenings. But the confusion and uncertainty in connection with this has been already shown. "Similar confusion," says Powell (p. 219), "is to be found in several succeeding parts." Platina, who had as good opportunity as any man to know the truth of history, as to the succession of the popes, etc., acknowledges that the authorities on the subject, in several of the following centuries, were full of confusion. "And he complains," says Prideaux, "that they who were appointed as *prothonotaries* to register the passages in the church were, in his time, become so illiterate that some of them could scarce write their own names in Latin." Fine chroniclers, on whose faithfulness and accuracy to place the existence of our Christianity! Prideaux remarks in another place, A. D. 858, that "Onuphrius, Platina, Ciaconius, complain much of the neglect of registering, and the confusion of their popes' lives, notwithstanding their succession is made such a convincing argument."

And there seems to be quite a diversity of statement among the prelates of the Church of Rome, nothwithstanding that Cardinal Baronius tells us that false pontiffs were intruded into the chair of St. Peter by sordid and abandoned women, and indignantly demands, "Who can affirm that men illegally intruded by bad women (*scortis*) were Roman pontiffs?" Yet a prominent Western prelate is reported as saying of the popes, at the recent Plenary Council held in Baltimore, Md.: "The line of her rulers, from Leo XIII back to Peter, is as clear and bright and uninterrupted as the American Presidential succession from George Washington down to Chester A. Arthur."

The Romish Bishop Purcell, of Cincinnati, Ohio, in his debate with the Rev. Mr. Campbell, in 1837, stated, in the most explicit terms, *that there were vacancies, breaks in the chain.* (Debate, p. 144.) Although the same man has said (Debate, p. 108), in speaking of the succession, "it has been faithfully noticed, and regularly perpetuated, in an unbroken chain of pontiffs down to the present chief pastor [Pius IX], auspiciously presiding over all the Church." However, like an old, experienced casuist, armed *cap-à-pie* for every emergency, he offers this as an escape from the dilemma, viz.: "The lapse of a few years, before binding together the links of the Apostolical Succession, does not affect the great principle" of that succession. "We are," he adds, "no believers in metempsychosis, or that, like the supposed divinity of the Lama of Thibet, the soul of a deceased pope goes, by a hop, skip, and jump, right off into his successor. We will wait six months or six years to find a good pope. If the pope were a poor wanderer in the mountains of the moon, it would not destroy his authority, though the See of Peter should be vacant for seventy years." (Debate, pp. 144–46, 154.) The question is not, however, how the soul of a dead pope is transferred to another, but how the *grace*, under the circumstances of "breaks in the chain," can be employed in the forging and welding together of a *new* link. What about the succession of the generation—in fact, two generations—of popes, prelates, and priests, raised up during the seventy years of the absence of the pope as a "poor wanderer" in the mountains of the moon, or anywhere else? And what means has Bishop Purcell, or has our prominent Western prelate, or have any of those in this boasted line of succession, of knowing whether their ordination is in a line perpetuated after the return of the "poor wanderer," or one extemporized during his unhappy absence? "Clear, bright, and uninterrupted!" Shades of St. Peter! Indeed, it looks very much, to an innocent looker-on, as if, in view of the confessed "breaks in the chain," the only channel, according to Romish theories, of communicating the functions apostolic—manual imposition of hands in unbroken descent—like the extinguished fluid of a demolished Leyden jar, is cut off,—a consideration of itself, I submit, decisive of the fallacy of the whole dogma in question.

(*3.*) *The numerous and serious schisms in the Papal Church, and the multiplicity of claimants to the Papal Chair at one and the same time.*

The lordly boast of the Roman organism as to its unity and peace is demonstrated to be fallacious by the facts cited by her own acknowledged historians.* They tell us of strange divisions and of stranger ways of healing them. One admits that, up to the fourteenth century, there had been more than twenty schisms in the popedom. Some of these were of the most serious character. One continued for forty years; another lasted during eighty years. Sometimes there were two, three, or four popes at the same time, each claiming to be the true pope, each

---

* For citations of authorities covering the discussion of these topics, see references in Section 10 of Powell on "Apostolical Succession." Also, Shimeall.

having his party, and each denouncing and excommunicating the others. Thus was the Church divided into the most ferocious factions. It is plain that when several assumed the office at the same time, all could not be genuine and legitimate claimants to the same chair. Only one could be the true and proper pope; all others were spurious and counterfeit. Through what channel was transmitted the pretended tactual succession of to-day? Did it come through the pope at Rome, Italy, or did it come through the pope at Avignon, France? Which really occupied the chair of St. Peter has never been settled, and no man on earth can tell. How were such schismatic difficulties settled? Once the Council of Constance deposed the three claiming popes. They were condemned as false popes, heretics, and ungodly wretches, not even to be reckoned in the number of Christians. Other and more summary ways were employed. Resort was had to poison and other forms of murder. Hildebrand (Gregory VII) poisoned six or seven popes, and then, without any election, thrust himself into the popedom. "Frequently the most cunning, the most powerful, the most warlike, or the most wicked of them succeeded in deposing his less cunning, less powerful, less warlike, or less wicked opponent. For the proofs of all that is here said, let the reader peruse Platina's

'Lives of the Popes,' Bishop Jewell's 'Apology,' and the 'Defense' of that 'Apology,' as well as many other authorities of a like nature. Now, who can trace the *true succession* when the whole Church was divided against itself—cardinals against cardinals, councils against councils, and nations against nations? Could factions and poison and murder and wars and bloodshed, which alone decided in these schisms, settle the true succession? Answer, ye modern boasters about your spiritual descent through this *unbroken* line." (Powell.) No wonder Cardinal Baronius should say: "In those days the Church indeed was, for the most part, *without a pope.*"

How any sane man can seriously pretend to find order, regularity, and apostolical succession from all these schisms passes my humble comprehension. I know not how to account for the putting forth of such claims, except on one or more of the three following suppositions: Either, first, that the men who assert these claims are ignorant of the facts of Church history; or, secondly, that they suppose that all other men are sufficiently ignorant to be imposed upon; or, thirdly, that they act upon the plan that those who make the most pretense will certainly carry the day. Let but the multiplied thousands of voices of those whom they call Dissenters and Protestants be raised, as they should, in one vast, solemn dissent, protest, and exposition against this pretense, and the strong and uncompromising voice of history thunder forth its overwhelming testimony, and the condemnation of arrogant assumption will be doubly assured.

In addition to the historical impossibility of a line of transmission through the Romish Church, there is a moral or spiritual consideration quite as insuperable; then,

(*4.*) *The moral, or, rather, the immoral character of many of the Popes.*

No amount of ecclesiastical pretense, or theological jugglery, can so varnish a bad man, who has waded to preferment through iniquity, as to make him appear either fit for heaven or to bear the authority in the Church, which he has obtained by violent methods. Did limits not forbid, I should here insert pages 228 to 237 from Powell on "Apostolical Succession," commending their reading. I select but a few illustrations, since that author asserts nothing but from authors of undisputed credit, cited in footnotes. He declares the popes to have been monsters in wickedness. Pope Vigilius waded to the pontifical throne through the blood of his predecessor. Pope Pelagius was obliged to clear himself of the suspicion of murdering Vigilius by swearing his innocence upon the crucifix and the Gospels. Boniface III obtained the popedom of Phocas, who had murdered Mauritius, the emperor, and had become emperor in his place. The Popes Constantine and Gregory II distinguished themselves in favor of image-worship. Pope Joan, they tell us, a female in disguise, was elected and confirmed as Pope John VIII, whose death was caused by the shameless amours to which she surrendered herself. The truth of this statement has, since the Reformation, been called in question as resting upon mere tradition; but tradition ought not to be objected to by those who make tradition the rule of faith. Besides, Pope Joan was no worse than many of the male popes. Unless her name stands as John VIII, there is a break in the catalogues of popes, as furnished by the successionists. Without her help they can not get back to their alleged Peter—can not continue her in their catalogues, and at the same time reject her. Dean Prideaux declares that there are fifty authorities belonging to the Church of Rome in favor of it; that is, who maintain that Joan, a female pope, actually was elected and inaugurated. Some learned Protestants have good-naturedly given up this history, and we need not contend about it. But the case seems to be about like this, as crisply stated by Rev. Dr. George Peck: "There is given in the chronicles to which recourse is had for the Romish succession, written by the priests and monks of the Church of Rome, credited and related by the high functionaries of that Church, archbishops and penitentiaries, and *universally* believed for the space of five hundred years, the name of a female pope—fictitious, if you please—who is said to have reigned about two and a half years, and *ordained* bishops! Thus we have the *quod ab omnibus* evidence for five centuries to a female link in the succession, which Catholics, *Roman* and *Anglican*, now laugh at as a fable of the monks." Now, let the reader not forget that it is to these very chroniclers that our successionists go to identify each link of the Romish succession for at least the space of eight centuries! Doubtless all their records, excepting that of "Dame Joan," "are as susceptible of proof as the genuineness and authenticity of the books of the New Testament"—successionists being the judges.

To me it seems as if given factitious circumstances may have been interwoven with the story of the *Popess* Joan. Yet it can not be destitute of all foundation. Certainly some unusual event must have happened at Rome from which this story has derived its origin; for it is not at all credible, from any principle of moral evidence, that an event should be universally believed and related in the same manner by a multitude of historians during five centuries immediately succeeding its proposed date, if that account was absolutely destitute of all foundation.

Many of the popes were heretics. Pope Liberius subscribed to Arianism. Marcellinus sacrificed to idols. Honorius was condemned and accursed for a heretic in two general councils. Leo was also an Arian heretic. Sylvester I was made pope by necromancy, and in recompense thereof promised both body and soul to the devil. Eugenius was condemned as a despiser of the Holy Canons. Prideaux numbers among the popes "thirty-eight usurping Nimrods, forty luxurious Sodomites, forty Egyptian magicians, forty-one devouring Abaddons, twenty incurable Babylonians." The authors of the Lives of the Popes make mention of multitudinous crimes among them that must not be mentioned on these pages. Yet these are the men who, even in this enlightened day, are dragged forth to the light as the successors of the apostles of Jesus Christ! It is through these same men—with all their filthiness, their simony, incest, and murders—that some men seek, in our time, to make an unbroken chain of succession to the apostle Peter. Shall we, in this day of grace, congratulate such upon their descent from spiritual ancestors so illustrious? No! no! Such congratulations would be but little, if any, short of cruel; for this line of popes seems certainly to record the legitimate successors of Herod and Pontius Pilate, Nero and Caligula, rather than the meek and lowly Jesus and his humble and spiritual-minded apostles. (For table of Legal Flaws in the Papal Succession, see "Petrine Claims," pp. 343–346.)

Now comes the question, How can sacramental virtue pass through the hands of these men and boys—for they were sometimes boys of ten and five years old—how can the essential vitality of the Church and ministry pass pure and good through such channels? I am aware that the advocates of the external successional theory adduce this formula; namely, the wickedness of the *person* does not prevent or obstruct the discharge of official duty by him; that the badness of the incumbent can not vitiate the office. One writer (Bishop Hobart) says: "The acts of a wicked magistrate, the decisions of a corrupt judge, are valid, *because of his commission.* The acts of unholy ministers in the Church are valid for the same reason, *because of their commission.*"

But the cases are by no means parallel. Immoralities, to a certain extent, in a judge will not, and to an extent beyond that they will, work as a nullity of his official acts, and disqualify for office.

Moreover, in what sense is the term "valid" used? Presumably, it means of legal, binding force. But upon whom is it binding? As to the Church and the bishop and the persons ordained, binding it may be. But that is not the whole question. *Is the act binding upon Christ?* The Lord Jesus binds himself to confer blessing in pursuance of certain promises. Now, do his promises say that the ministrations of a wicked man will be recognized by him, and that in and through them he will confer his blessings? Does he not, then, rather disown both the men and their acts, and declare his unceasing curses and displeasure upon them? We have already conceded that an ordination performed by a wicked bishop may be binding upon the ordained man and the Church, for the reason that they entered into the arrangement in good faith; *the ordination being,* let it be noted, *a matter between the Church and the minister.* The validity of the ordination, if valid at all, is not because of any vitality or sacramental virtue personal in the bishop, and which is conferred by him as the vicar of Christ, but because of the good faith in which the Church and the minister to be ordained entered into the matter. The ordained minister is the minister of the Lord Jesus Christ, and not of the bishop. There is something more than the absurd in the idea that men, monstrously wicked—who did not so much as know whether there be any Holy Ghost, and therefore not under his influence—should be able to communicate spiritual blessings and spiritual authority, and to impart the Holy Spirit to others. Can it be true that an ordination is absolutely valid "because of the commission" of the bishop? Let us see: Suppose a man to go to a validly ordained bishop, and offer a thousand dollars for ordination, and the ceremony is performed. Is the man a "valid" bishop? Or, suppose him to go with a revolver, and, under its persuasions, demand the ceremony of ordination, and procure it. Is he a bishop? The "commission" was certainly not lacking in the ordainer, and you, who will, say that in either event there is an ordination recognized by the Lord Jesus Christ. Allow this doctrine of conferring "valid" orders by the virtue of personal "commission," and we might have a Christian Church and ministry without a Christian in it. What a solecism! Suppose a modern Liberal League were, in some way, to procure ordination for one of their number to the presbyterate or to the bishopric; according to the theory of conferring valid orders by virtue of personal "commission," that clan immediately becomes a Christian Church. There is no evasion of the logic of that. If Satan and his host incarnate should become ordained by succession bishops, on this theory the ordinances they might administer would possess sacramental grace. On such a basis, too, if those thus ordained and possessing "the succession," should decline to place ordaining hands on other heads, there would be no valid, efficacious ministry in the world, when the present generation of ministers shall have passed away, and thus the adversary of human souls would have the race vanquished and at his mercy. Is it reasonable for a moment to suppose that the Holy Spirit would thus suspend the perpetuation of his own institutions on the will or whim of fallible, not to say of basely wicked, mortals? that the great Head of the Church has tied his own hands? No! no!

I know that it is averred that, if the Lord has chosen this method of perpetuating his Church, he will see that it is done. To this theory we will pay our compliments later. (See Section 4, Objection the Third.) If this doctrine—that bad men could not vitiate the succession—be true, then the Lord Jesus affords his direct sanction to the ministrations of bad men, whatever errors they may teach and whatever may be the enormity of their crimes. Can any man reconcile this revolting principle with the solemn and express declarations of God's own Word? Christianity is eminently a holy religion. It calls upon all men, everywhere, to repent and do works meet for repentance. The sacrament of holy baptism, by which men are inducted into the Church, teaches them most impressively that, from the very beginning of their Christian course, they are to cleanse themselves from all moral filthiness, and walk in newness of life. Every one that names the name of Christ is to depart from iniquity, and deny himself of all ungodliness and worldly lusts; he is to live soberly, righteously, and godly, in all good conscience, before God and man. Indeed, "if any man have not the spirit of Christ, he is none of his."

The Christian ministry, the most sacred and responsible of all offices that either man or angel can sustain, is not made any exception. And yet men have the audacity to declare, in effect, that the valid exercise of its functions is consistent with every form of impiety and wickedness! What presumption! Without a syllable of authority from his Word, the Head of the Church is daringly pledged to approve and bless the official acts of men guilty of that against which he has uttered the most awful denunciations of his vengeance; because, forsooth, they are in the lineal descent of an imaginary succession through the self-styled primates of the Church! That the Lord may, and often does, overrule for good the doings of wicked men, is cheerfully conceded; but it is impossible that the ministration of such should have his sanction. Psalm l, 16, 17: "Unto the wicked God saith, What hast thou to do that thou shouldst take my covenant into thy mouth, seeing thou hatest instruction and castest my word behind thee?" Matt. vii, 15, 16, 20: "Beware of false prophets which come to you in sheep's clothing, but inwardly they are ravening wolves. Ye shall know them by their fruits. Do men gather grapes of thorns, or figs of thistles? Wherefore, by their fruits ye shall know them." If the grand test of a man's ministerial authority be the nature of his ordination, how could our Lord direct the people to judge of it by personal conduct?

"No man is a true minister of Christ who is not commissioned by him, but Christ never commissions any man who is not a sincere Christian; yet many of the popes, we see, were wicked men, as were multitudes of prelates ordained by them; therefore, many of the popes, and multitudes of the prelates ordained by them, were mere intruders into the sacred office, and not true ministers of Christ. Take away these spurious links, and where is the chain? Those who are wanting in the qualifications specified in the inspired Canons (1 Tim. iii; Titus i), are ineligible to the office of a bishop; but many popes, and multitudes of prelates ordained by them, lacked every qualification there specified; therefore, many popes, and multitudes of prelates ordained by them, were intruders into the sacred office, and not true ministers of Christ. Take away these spurious links, and where is the chain? In numerous canons of councils, recognized especially by Romanists and Anglicans, it is declared that none can be true ministers of Christ who are immoral, heretical, schismatical, simoniacal, nonaged, or saltant; but many popes, and multitudes of prelates ordained by them, have been notoriously in this category; therefore, papists and prelates themselves being judges, many popes and multitudes of prelates were intruders into the sacred office, and not true ministers of Christ. Take away these spurious links, and where is the chain." (Summers.) He who will read the lives of the popes will find scarcely one who gave evidence of a renewed nature, from Gregory the Great, sometimes styled the last good and the first bad pope, to Leo X, who flourished at the time of the Reformation, and who is reputed as an infidel.

It is in vain to say that Judas was a bad man, and that he was put by Christ into the college of apostles; and that, therefore, a valid ministry may exist in the persons of wicked men. The case of Judas is totally misapprehended. If it could be shown that Judas acted as a minister of Jesus Christ while he was a traitor, and the Savior recognized his acts of ministry after he betrayed his Lord, the case would be different. But what were the facts? Was Judas a bishop?

Was he a minister of the gospel? Was he ever authorized to preach the gospel, or to ordain others to do so? Why, the ministry of the gospel was not authorized to be preached in the lifetime of Judas; he was dead before the apostolic commission was given! In all probability he never heard, understandingly, of a gospel or its ministry. He did not live in the gospel dispensation. Christ had neither shed his blood for sinners, nor had he risen from the dead, until after the death of this betrayer. Whatever else may be said of this celebrated sinner, this much must be said, that he lived and died *before the gospel ministry began.*

This argument can not be answered by saying that the Savior sent the twelve apostles forth to preach, in his life-time, with Judas among them. This is very true; but what the character of that preaching was, we do not certainly know. It was probably a forewarning of the forthcoming of the gospel. The gospel in its full development, the atonement, the crucified and risen Savior, the salvation of Jesus Christ based upon his death and resurrection, could not, in the nature of the case, be preached until after the death of Christ. The religious preaching before this looked forward to these events. The twelve apostles, however, did not fully preach these things, even prospectively, for they did not clearly understand them. They were hard to convince of his resurrection, even after it took place. The Christian dispensation commenced, not at the birth, but at the death of Jesus Christ. His death and resurrection form the corner-stone of Christianity.

And again, suppose, for a single moment, that Judas was a Christian apostle in the sense of a bishop. Then, his "commission" authorized him to ordain, and a chain of ordinations descending from him would be equally valid with that coming from John or Peter. Will that do? Is the Christianity of Judas "valid" Christianity? Those who claim him as a valid ordainer of Christian bishops have really no means of knowing but that they themselves may be *his successors!* Will this do? And yet it is the argument with which prelatical writers furnish us.

It is likewise a mere evasion to say that, if it be true that wickedness renders nugatory the ministrations of ministers or priests, that then all the ministrations of hypocritical and bad men, who may officiate at the Church altars, are invalid; and that, hence, no one can know when he has been baptized, or has communed, etc.; for, the Lord be thanked, we do not have to depend upon uncertainties. The efficacy of the sacraments depends not upon the punctilios of the outward *form*, nor upon the dubious *intention* of some officiating priest or minister—for, in such an event as that, we could not know, sure enough, whether we had been baptized or communed—but upon the promised blessing and presence of the Savior, in the measure of the receptive spiritual conditions of the participant, according to their faith. And thus we are met by Him at the baptismal font, or at the sacramental chancel, and granted the refreshing tokens of His love and favor; while those whose wickedness is exposed are ecclesiastically condemned, so that they walk no more with us. If a succession has been maintained through any and all moral delinquency, it has been done by a series of miracles of a kind which challenges the whole divine polity, not only in its material, but its moral order.

When I recall how the rival possessors of the mysterious virtue, which it is claimed inheres in the so-called unbroken succession, have superseded each other by cabals, bloody conflicts, and assassinations—men who were steeped in sensuality, and who spread desolation through extensive districts with a fiend-like avidity, and yet who pretend to have unfailingly possessed and transmitted that virtue in all its purity and power, simply and solely by the fact that a certain form called ordination was performed by some ecclesiastical officer—I can not wonder, I am bound to say, that many men, who have not risen to an apprehension of the higher and purer plane of thinking, as set forth farther on, have turned aside to infidelity, and have scorned the faith which would array itself in such absurdity and monstrosity. I know no way for it more effectually to expose itself to the ridicule of mankind than by such antiquated and preposterous assumptions.

Those who would say, What difference does it make whether the Romanists hold to the doctrine of transmissionism or not?—it would be well to remind that this is the strategic point in their line, the point of their gigantic power over multiplied millions of souls, the basis of their arrogant assumptions. Many of their theological doctrines, against which much is said, are so palpably absurd that they would cease to be powerful were they not harnessed to the hierarchical system which is impelled by the force of the dogma in consideration. The importance, therefore, of the foregoing considerations is apparent.

The papal claim is unsustained, ay, unsustainable; and, according to Scripture and historical facts, it appears to be the flimsiest pretense and the most unsubstantial figment that ever darkened the human imagination or that ever nightmared a human soul. What could have been in the mind of the great apostle when he penned 2 Corinthians xi, 13: "For such are false apostles, deceitful workers, transforming themselves into the apostles of Christ."

Section II.

IS THE DOCTRINE OF TRANSMISSION DEMONSTRABLE THROUGH THE EASTERN, OR GREEK CHURCH, AS IT IS COMMONLY CALLED?

The history of this, as a separate body, does not begin until the interruption of ecclesiastical communion between the pope at Rome and the patriarch at Constantinople, who excommunicated each other; the completed schism taking place A. D. 1054, since which time all attempts at reunion have utterly failed, and the schism is irreconcilable. No two Churches, Dr. Schaff declares, are so much alike in their creed, polity, and *cultus* as the Greek and Roman, and yet no two are such irreconcilable rivals, perhaps for the very reason of their affinity. Organically, they seem to have been a unit in the first seven councils, adopted their ritual and doctrinal decisions, and stood shoulder to shoulder in the ancient conflict with paganism and heresy. The schism seems to have grown out of doctrinal differences, and the aggressions of the papal monarchy which had developed, and the establishment of the Western Empire in connection therewith. It seems plain that, to all the difficulties in the way of transmissionism in the Latin Church, as shown in the previous section, it is subject in the Greek Church up to the date of the schism. Moreover, the government of the Greek Church being a patriarchal oligarchy—with patriarchs at Constantinople, Alexandria, Antioch, and Jerusalem, equal in rights, though the first named has a primacy of honor—would be far less able through the centuries to transmit a tactual succession than the Roman monarchy, which, with all its solidity, it has failed to do. The burden of proof may again be left where it properly belongs.

Section III.

IS THE DOCTRINE OF TRANSMISSION DEMONSTRABLE THROUGH THE ANGLICAN, OR THE ESTABLISHED, CHURCH OF ENGLAND?

That such is the claim as set forth in the words of the eminent Rev. Dr. Hook, formerly vicar of Leeds, England, whose sermon on "Hear the Church" is received as a representative statement, says: "The prelates who at the present time rule the Churches of these realms—that is, England—were validly ordained by others, who, by means of an unbroken spiritual descent of ordination, derived their mission from the apostles and from our Lord. This *continued descent is evident to every one* who chooses to investigate it. Let him read the catalogues of bishops ascending up to the most remote period. Our ordinations descend in a direct, unbroken line from Peter and Paul, the apostles of the circumcision, and to the Gentiles. Those great apostles successively ordained Linus, Cletus, and Clement, Bishops of Rome; and the apostolic succession was regularly continued from them to Celestine, Gregory, and Vitalianus, who ordained Patrick bishop of the Irish, and Augustine and Theodore for the English; and from those times an uninterrupted series of valid ordinations has carried down the Apostolic Succession in our Churches to the present day. There is not a bishop, priest, or deacon among us who can not, if he please, trace his own spiritual descent from St. Peter or St. Paul." Now, can this claim be sustained? There are, certainly, insurmountable difficulties in the way of such a possibility:

First, the English Church was excommunicated by the Roman. This will not be denied as an historic fact, occurring in the reign of Henry VIII, about the year 1531. For what reason, the papist and Protestant transmissionist have ever disagreed; the former averring it to be the righteous refusal of Pope Clement VII to divorce "Bluff Harry" from his lawful wife, Catherine of Aragon—said to be much his senior—that he might marry the beautiful and accomplished Anne Boleyn. The latter declare the act of the pope not to have been a matter of conscience, but one of policy—Catherine being related to Charles V, Emperor of Germany. The former declare Henry to have forced the ecclesiastics to take part by threats and persecutions, and to have obtained the forced approbation of such bishops as went with him, through the statutes of "Præmunire"— *i. e.*, the offense of introducing foreign authority, and intended to depress the civil power of the pope in the kingdom—long disregarded, but still of legal force in the realm; and that their self-justification, by echoing the German cry of reformation from the corruption in religion and the enormity of ecclesiastical power in exercise by the papacy, was wholly an afterthought; that Henry had resisted the principles of Luther and the other Reformers most vehemently, and that he had written a book against the principles of the Reformation and in favor of the papacy, as a reward for which Pope Leo X conferred upon him the honorary title of "Defender of the Faith"—a title, singularly enough, continued by the sovereigns of England to this day.

But, leaving the papist and Protestant transmissionists to proceed with their long and wordy war, we note that the papal bull of excommunication was declared, previous to which the Church in England had not been known as the Church of England. Now, the Church of Rome was or else was not the, or a, true Church, those interested, of course, making their own selection, by which they should cheerfully abide. It is well known to be a settled *principle in English* High-

Churchism that *the Romish ordinations are valid.* Conceding, then, as she does, that the papal is a true Church, the English Church confronts the difficulty that, on her own theory, the excommunication was valid, stands in full force, is recorded in heaven, and ratified by Christ as his own act. Such is the meaning of excommunication in papistic and High-Church theories. The effect, then, of excommunication is to put the party excommunicated out of the Church, to make him as a heathen man and a publican, having no part with Christ, no Church standing, no ordinances, no ministrations. All such are aliens from the Church of Christ. They are, most emphatically, left to " the uncovenanted mercies of God."

This excommunication against the Church of England by that of Rome stands in full force at this day, and those ecclesiastics who recognize the priests of the Church of Rome as validly ordained, even if destitute of a true religious life, while refusing to recognize ordained Christian ministers as lawfully ordained, though they may possess a true religious life, have this to comfort them as the logical sequence: that they thereby acknowledge the full force of this actual excommunication. Here, then, on the supposition that the papal is the true Church, is an effectual estoppel put upon Church of England claims to the doctrine of transmission.* Rome snapped the chain. There is a link broken—a link that has never been mended. The Church of England can go back to the reign of Henry VIII; but there she comes to a dead halt.

Feeling the full force of the awkwardness of the situation, English High-Church ecclesiastics have employed their best talent to make a historic showing by which to avoid Rome, attempting to show that a Church was planted at a very early day in Lyons, in ancient Gaul, now France. Then they have some historic fables that, at a very early day, it was introduced among the savages of Britain. Some even admit a tale of romance respecting St. Paul's visit to England, where he planted the gospel and ordained a "bishop;" that the apostolic succession was preserved in that island, in the See of Canterbury, whence it was also transferred to the United States a few years ago. But he who will patiently "box the compass" in noting the meanderings of the interested parties to dodge "Old Rome," whether by way of Ephesus, through St. John; of Alexandria, through St. Mark; of Antioch, through St. John or St. Peter; of Jerusalem, through St. James; of Syria, through St. Thomas; of Scotland, through Aidan; of Ire-

---

*This lies with equal force against any others who may depend on Rome for tracing authentic visibility.

land, through St. Columba; of Canterbury, "in a threefold cord not quickly broken," through Saints Paul, John, and Peter,—will, at the last, be brought back again to Augustin, the first Saxon bishop and the first archbishop of Canterbury. (See "End of Prelacy," ch. vi.)

Let us remember that there was a reformation of the Church in the sixteenth century, by which the Protestants broke off from the Romish communion and set up a Christian Church. Previous to the Reformation, the whole of Christianity was under the dominion of the Church of Rome, except a handful of persecuted refugee Christians, here and there, in the forests and mountains of France, Germany, and Switzerland. (Heaven be thanked for these! A true civilization and a pure Christianity owes much to them.) But all of known public organized Christianity in the world was, for a whole thousand years, under the Romish dominion, except the Oriental Churches, from which their succession could not and is not claimed to have been derived. A part of the Romish Church was in Africa, part in Germany, part in Switzerland, part in France, part in Scotland, *and a part in England.* What matters it how early the Church was planted in England, or by whom? It is well known that since the visit of Augustin to that country, in A. D. 596, up to the declaration of independence of the Church by Henry VIII, in 1531, a period of nearly a thousand years, the only organized Church in the island of Great Britain was a regular Roman Catholic Church. Why, in her " Homily against the Peril of Idolatry," the Church of England herself declares: "Laity and clergy, learned and unlearned, *all ages, sects, and degrees of men, women, and children* of the whole of Christendom, had been at once drowned in abominable idolatry, and that for the *space of eight hundred years and more.*" The fact is, the original owners of those dioceses had been extinct for centuries, having been principally destroyed by the army of Ethelbert, or Æthelberht, king of Kent, and they had left no successors. The popish line superseded the British, and the latter did not *coalesce* with, but was *annihilated* by, the former. It is not necessary for a Church of Rome to be *in the city of Rome.* "There was more Romish faith in London than in the Vatican." (D'Aubigné, Hist. Ref., Vol. V, p. 189.) And it is not known that the *corruptions* of Rome were ever circumscribed by any geographical or other boundaries. For what purpose apostolical successionists attempt to set up a line of ordinations separate and apart from, and independent of, Rome is not very apparent. If Romish ordinations are invalid, then what invalidates them according to High-Church doctrine? That view claims that ordinations are valid "because of the commission" of the ordaining bishop, irrespective of any morality or immorality, piety or impiety, in the bishop personally. Then what invalidates Romish ordinations? If they are not invalid, then are they not as good as validity can make them? *Why*, then, the anxious effort to make history of uncertain things in order to get rid of it? If this successionism is not good in the Romish Church, then how *can* it be good in any other? The thing is plainly impossible. Taking hold, then, of this horn of the dilemma, that the Romish is a true Church, the Church of England finds herself hopelessly excommunicated. Now, if the Romish bishops, at the time of the English reformation, had the exclusive authority to administer in the Churches derived by a succession of commissions, then those who preached at all must do it in obedience to this authority. But some of them *protested*, and hence became Protestants. They, therefore, threw off and repudiated the binding force of authority derived in that way. After they became Protestants, they preached, of course, if they preached at all, in virtue of some other authority than that against which they protested; for it is clear that a man can not solemnly renounce his connection with a Church—any Church—and after that preach and exercise ministerial functions in virtue of the authority thus renounced. Can it be presumed for a moment by any that official authority or power may be lawfully exercised in spite of the authority which lawfully and properly conferred it? This is supposing that two lawful things may lawfully oppose and fight and destroy each other, or that lawful and unlawful are the same. They were all excommunicated by the papal authority; hence the Church of England can not possess a transmitted succession.

Now turn to the other alternative; namely, that the Church of Rome is not the Church. She had no authority from Christ to excommunicate; it was not done in his name nor by his authority; he has not ratified it. Rome can become so corrupt as no longer to be the true Church. If so, then it is vain to attempt a passage to the apostles along that road; for we come to a place where Rome has ceased to be a true Church, and at that spot we are at the end of our chain; the succession is broken; there is no road cut through that dismal swamp. Lord Macaulay, the great English historian, and a man who ought to know, says: "It is probable that no clergyman of the Church of England can trace up his spiritual genealogy from bishop to bishop even so far back as the time of the Reformation." Again: "It is as impossible for a minister of our day to prove that he is in direct succession as to prove that he is lineally descended from Ahab and Jezebel."

The *second* great difficulty in the way of regularly transmitted ministerial or apostolic succession through the establishment is the *political* rather than religious character of its inception. King Henry VIII, although a mere unordained layman, proclaimed himself as the head of the English Church, and cut off all connection between his subjects and Rome, thus changing, in its entirety, the constitution of the Church in England; thus, too, casting the Church in entire and helpless dependence upon a kingdom of this world; making it the mere child of the State; vesting all authority in ecclesiastical matters in the reigning sovereign, as the statute-books affirm, the bishops even receiving their commissions from the king or queen, a sort of power of attorney to act for him or her. The sovereign has power to commission laymen both to preach and ordain if he may so wish; he may direct what doctrines may or may not be preached, or he may forbid all preaching; he has the power of discipline. It is said that the identical powers which the law and constitution gave to Henry VIII, in matters pertaining to the Church, were renewed in the reign of Edward VI, and also of Elizabeth, and that they continue to be the law of the Church of England to this day. Those who desire a full and yet succinct statement of this whole case, with proper authorities cited in proof, such as Lingard's "History of the Time," and many others, will do well to read chapter xiv, "The Church of England the Mere Child of the State," in "The Trials of a Mind in its Progress to Catholicism," by L. Silliman Ives, LL. D., at one time Protestant Episcopal Bishop of North Carolina, but who, in 1854, became a pervert to the Roman Catholic faith, and who can not, therefore, be prejudiced against the doctrine of transmission.

With those who fancy that they can secure an apostolic succession, transmitted through a political line, we could not wish to dispute, and readily recognize that much Christian piety has proceeded through this line in spite of its secular character; but for ourselves, we have no use for a chain of apostolic succession which is hung on a political hook driven into the wall by such a man as Henry VIII. We are not aware that the apostles would claim any relationship to him. Is it said there is always a relation between the Church and the State, we reply, But there is a most decided difference between a State Church ruled by the State, subject to king and Parliament, and a Church in the State ruled by its own laws, and subject to neither king nor Parliament, President nor Congress. The history of the Church of England, from first to last, is a history of the politics of England, ecclesiastically considered. The Church corporation of England is, in every respect, as absolutely a creature of the laws of England as the University of Oxford, and, being a civil institution for political purposes, is about as apostolical an institution as the monarch or the aristocracy of England. Those identified with the Church of England, or who depend upon it for supposed favors, aver that, though in union with the State, it yet has some sort of independent existence. Previous to the Reformation, the Church there had a substantive being of its own. It had power, which it professed to derive from Christ through the Roman See, and with which the State might not intermeddle; but at the Reformation the Church was absorbed into the State, and from that time to this the "Establishment" has been as completely a part of the State, as entirely a creature of the law, as is the army and navy, or the East India Company. "The truth is," says a writer, "the Church of England since the Reformation is an Erastian establishment from the foundation to the topstone. The same legislative power which, within a few years past, has abolished so many bishoprics in Ireland [this was some forty years ago], may reduce all the bishoprics to one, and may then suppress that one; or it may multiply them till every parish has a bishop of its own, and then organize them into classical, provincial, and national assemblies, with lay delegates intermixed. It may abolish the Articles, the Creeds, the surplice, or the Liturgy; or it may translate the Prayer-book back into Latin, command the adoration of the wafer, and restore the supremacy of the chair to St. Peter.

In speaking of the doctrine of successionism, Hallam, the historian, says, "The first traces of the doctrine are found about the end of the Elizabethan reign," which calls to mind events at the re-Protestantizing of the Church of England under Queen Elizabeth, after the horrible reign of the Roman Catholic Queen Mary, at the alleged ordination of Matthew Parker as Archbishop of Canterbury, and the affair at Nag's Head. The Roman Catholic account runs thus: All the consecration that Parker, the first Protestant Archbishop of Canterbury, ever had was performed at the Nag's Head Tavern, a kind of resort for rural ministers. Thus Bishop Bonner, being then by order of Elizabeth in prison, having heard of the intention then and there to consecrate Parker, sent his chaplain, an eminent scholar by the name of Neal, to witness the ceremony. Among these consecrators the only consecrated bishop was Kitchin, who alone, of all the Roman Catholic bishops, had saved his miter by taking the oath of supremacy. Bonner sent by Neal a menace to Kitchin, that, if he took part in the consecration, he should be excommunicated; and Kitchin took no share, leaving Parker destitute of canonical orders. The proof of this story is the statement of Neal, and a public statement of the fact in Parliament by the Bishop of Durham, in defense of Parker's canonicity. Years after the Bishop of Durham denied that he ever made such a statement in Parliament; but Lord Audley, a member of the House of Lords, replied by public letter that he himself heard the statement made by the good bishop. (See "The Validity of Anglican Ordinations and Anglican Claims to Apostolical Succession, Examined by Peter Richard Kenrick, Archbishop of St. Louis.")

The Anglicans, of course, deny this story by saying, "It was a calumny, to which the custom of the newly ordained bishops furnishing a grand dinner or entertainment gave rise." They declare the ordination to have taken place at Lambeth Palace, and that then adjournment to the Nag's Head for supper took place. This would not, however, affect the facts as to whom the consecrators may or may not have been; nor could the place, however inappropriate, vitiate the acts which there took place, nor any authority there properly conveyed. A strong defense of the legitimacy of Parker's consecration is made in "Sermons to Presbyterians of all Sects," by G. T. Chapman, D. D., pp. 305–314. On page 309, quoting from Lingard's History as his strong tower, he says: "Barlow, Scorey, Coverdale, and Hodgkins, suffragan of Bedford, confirmed the election on the ninth and consecrated Parker on the seventeenth (*i. e.*, Dec., 1559). The ceremony was performed, though with a little variation, according to the ordinal of Edward VI. Two of the consecrators (Barlow and Hodgkins) had been ordained bishops according to the Roman pontifical; the other two according to the reformed ordinal." Thus it seems that, from the very strongest defense possible, the Anglican transmissionists must depend for their succession upon a ceremony half Protestant and half popish, with the latter half performed without canonical authority—since a deposed bishop loses his rights—and under interdiction at that. Let those who can believe that through Parker, by reason of this consecration, "the legitimate priesthood has descended to our times?"—as says Dr. Chapman—be content therewith. As for ourselves, we can not receive any such contradictory absurdity. No wonder, in view of this and many of the accompanying events, the Roman Catholic *World* in June, 1880 (quoted in *Methodist Quarterly Review*, October, 1880, p. 735), in reviewing the arguments of the Anglicans against the apostolicity of our youngest sister, the Reformed Episcopal Church, concludes that whatever argument they may use in that direction, lodges, logically and historically, against themselves. However, leaving the parties to that controversy to fight their paper battle, we may be permitted to conclude that Parker's consecration can not be, as it ought to be, considered clearly and satisfactorily proven. To us it is ecclesiastically an unimportant question. For the Anglican Church can be just as valid a Church with Parker unconsecrated as consecrated, if she so order, because it is the mandate of the covenanted brotherhood. However, to those who for salvation must "hear the Church," and who hold that a successional ordination is the test of a valid Church, the question of Parker's ordination is a vital point. "Upon that thread hangs the whole Anglican Church. It is by this partition of very thin film that they are rescued from Romanism." In the work of Mr. Haddan, already referred to, many pages are given to show the canonical ordination of Parker; but the misfortune of that author is in being compelled to draw almost wholly on such sources of information as Parker himself had to do with; it has, therefore, about the force of an accused party attempting also to be the judge and jury. Whether Archbishop Parker was or was not truly ordained at Lambeth by Bishop Barlow in pursuance of the queen's commission, and whether Barlow was or was not truly ordained by a bishop, and whether this whole famous Nag's Head procedure was or was not all that is alleged for it by successionists, certain it is, the ordinations were not performed in pursuance of the authority of the Church of Rome—then in power in England—and upon which the Anglicans depended for a succession, if they could get it at all.

No wonder Macaulay, himself one of the most distinguished members of the Church of England and who will not be charged with sectarian bias, said, in his celebrated review of Gladstone's "Church and State," republished in his "Miscellanies," after demanding the evidence for the alleged fact of apostolical succession in the Church of England: "The transmission of orders from the apostles to an English clergyman of the present day, must have been through a very great number of intermediate persons. Now, it is probable that no clergyman in the Church of England can trace up his spiritual genealogy, from bishop to bishop, even so far back as the time of the Reformation. There remain fifteen or sixteen hundred years, during which the history of the transmission of orders is buried in utter darkness. And whether he be priest by succession from the apostles, depends on the question whether, during that long period, some thousands of events took place, any one of which may, without any gross improbability, be supposed not to have taken place. We have not a tittle of evidence to any one of these events. We do not even know the names or countries of the men to whom it is taken for granted that these events happened. We do not know whether the spiritual ancestors of any one of our contemporaries were Spanish or Armenian, Arian or Orthodox. In the utter absence of all particular evidence, we are surely entitled to require that the strictest regularity was observed in every generation, and that episcopal functions were exercised by none who were not bishops by succession from the apostles. But we have no such evidence. In the first place, we have not full and accurate information touching the polity of the Church during the century which followed the persecution of Nero. The question whether the primitive ecclesiastical constitution bore a greater resemblance to the Anglican or the Calvinistic model, has been fiercely disputed. It is a question on which at least a full half of the ability and erudition of Protestant Europe has, ever since the Reformation, been opposed to the Anglican pretensions. Our author himself, we are persuaded, would have the candor to allow that if no evidence were admitted but that which is furnished by the genuine Christian literature of the first two centuries, judgment would not go in favor of prelacy"—that is, transmissionism.

Section IV.

IS THE DOCTRINE OF TRANSMISSION DEMONSTRABLE BY THE ANGLO-AMERICAN, OR PROTESTANT EPISCOPAL, CHURCH?

That this body received, properly and validly, all that the Church of England had to bestow, may be cheerfully admitted; that it could receive more, can not consistently be claimed.

Antecedent to the American Revolution, the Church of England Churches in the Colonies were administered as a part of the diocese of the Bishop of London, but after the successful culmination of that struggle, and the recognition of the independence of the Colonies in 1783, that part of the jurisdiction of that dignitary was of course at an end.

Beginning as early as the spring of the year 1784, conventions were held in different States, preliminary to organization "independent of all foreign authority, ecclesiastical or civil." "These minor conventions, in separate States, voted for a representation of the clergy and laity to meet in New York in October, 1784, where delegates from eight different States were convened."* "In

---

*These quotations and dates are from "Genius and Mission of the Protestant Episcopal Church in the United States," by Rev. Calvin Colton, LL. D.

October, 1785, the General Convention of the Protestant Episcopal Church in the United States was organized." "The constitution of the Church was matured by a committee appointed by this convention, and adopted by the convention of 1789." That Church was not fully authorized to exercise the full powers of an independent body until 1790, when Rev. J. Madison, D. D., a clergyman of Virginia, was consecrated to the episcopal office by the Archbishop of Canterbury. For, though in 1787 the Rev. William White, of Pennsylvania, and the Rev. Samuel Provost, of New York, were consecrated bishops of the American Church by the two archbishops of England, assisted by the bishop of Bath and Wells and by the bishop of Peterborough, they were not allowed to consecrate others to the episcopal office until there were three regular bishops, constituted such by receiving their ordination from the hands of the English bishops. During the interim there was no bond of unification, no general organization, and no bishop; and, if "no bishop no Church" be true, as alleged by transmissionism, then the Protestant Episcopal Church did not exist until A. D. 1790. It is true that Rev. Dr. Seabury, who had been elected by the Church of England Churches in Connecticut to be their bishop, received, November 14, 1784, the imposition of hands in the Episcopal Church of Scotland—known popularly as the Jacobite, or Nonjuring Church. The succession in that body runs back to James II; the English Church, however, regarded it as schismatic and did not recognize its acts, and it in turn regarded the English revolution of William and Mary (1689) as only successful rebellion. Dr. Seabury did not come into authority in his diocese in Connecticut until August, 1789, when he acted with the other bishops in the consecration of Rev. T. Claggett, D. D., as bishop of Maryland—the first Protestant Episcopal bishop consecrated in America.

But of course, as already suggested, the maintenance of transmissionism in this body must rest with the Established Church of England.

The references to historic facts in this section are made with all possible deference to the Christian body named.

Section V.

IS THE DOCTRINE OF TRANSMISSIONISM DEMONSTRABLE BY WAY OF THE *UNITAS FRATRUM* (UNITED BRETHREN), OR MORAVIAN, CHURCH?

This body[*] is a relic of the ancient Slavonian Churches, which have a history from the ninth century, and the evangelization of Central Eu-

---

[*] The *Unitas Fratrum*, or Moravians, must not be—as it is sometimes—confounded with the denomination of United Brethren in Christ. John Lawrence, in his history of the latter people, after a long review of the his-

rope, by missionaries belonging to the Greek Church of those days. Notwithstanding the sea of tribulations through which they and their countrymen had passed, certain evangelical Churches of Moravia and Bohemia, confederated under the title of the Unity of the Brethren (*Unitas Fratrum*), survived till the sixteenth century, and reckoned their adherents by the thousands. But, as usual, the iron grip of the papacy was felt. The liberties of the Bohemian nation, and the evangelical faith in Bohemia and Moravia, after untold horrors, protracted through several generations, were suppressed. The Church of the United Brethren was no longer to be seen. The ancient tree was utterly cast down. In 1722

---

tory of the Waldenses, the United Brethren, the Mennonites, the Renewed United Brethren, or *Unitas Fratrum*—drawing largely upon "History of the Protestant Church of the United Brethren," by Rev. John Holmes, printed in London, 1825, says, (Vol. I, p. 91): "The Renewed United Brethren had had no *ecclesiastical* connection with the original United Brethren, as the original United Brethren had none with the Waldenses;" although possessing a life-connection through Christ in all things essential to the being and prosperity of a true Christian Church. Nor does he claim more for the Church of which he is historian, as he shows its evolution from remnants of the Brethren from Europe, scattered among the Germans in the Colonies; and from the German Reformed by way of the Evangelical Reformed Church, at the head of which had been the apostolic and seraphic Otterbein (pp. 246, *et al.*)

a small band of these evangelical Moravians—who had secretly cherished the evangelical faith of their fathers and who remembered, doubtless, the polity of the ancient Unity—crossed the borders into Saxony, and at Hernnhut found a refuge, and in Count Zinzendorf a patron. They had the evangelical succession of doctrine and faith, although the external tactual succession of manual imposition was gone—if, indeed, it ever existed. Bishop E. De Schweinitz, of the Moravian Church, says (see "Schaff-Herzog Encyclopedia of Religious Knowledge," art. Moravian Church) that body is a resuscitation, in a new form, of the Bohemian Brethren. Of the Bohemian Brethren their own historian (G. Von Zezschwitz) says (see *ibid.*, art. Bohemian Brethren): "The general outline of the history of this sect is perfectly clear. . . . Its birth—however its relation to Rokyczana and the Utraquists on the one side, and to the Waldenses on the other—is still somewhat obscure." The Utraquists were the followers of the Bohemian reformer and martyr, John Huss, of the fifteenth century; and Rokyczana was one of the principal controversialists in the contest with the papacy. The Waldenses were a body of dissenters from the hateful features of the papal Church, and arose in Lyons in the twelfth century.

Thus it seems that transmissionism is not here

demonstrable; but, as is usual, is left in "obscurity" and to conjecture.

Section VI.

IS THE DOCTRINE OF TRANSMISSION DEMONSTRABLE BY WAY OF THE CULDEE CHURCH?

That Christianity was introduced into Scotland very near to, if not during, the lives of the apostles, seems to be quite in evidence, and, too, from an Asiatic and not from a European source; from the Churches ministered to by Paul and John, and not from the Church at Rome. The primitive Church of the Culdees was first established on the Scottish island of Iona, and from thence spread to the main-land. "The gallant struggle of the old Culdee Church with the gigantic power of Rome began about A. D. 650. It continued until the establishment of popery by David I, in A. D. 1150, and, indeed, for some time afterward; for the final overthrow did not take place until the suppression of the Culdees of St. Andrews, A. D. 1297." (Moore.) The historian declares that "all those means by which a religious body may be *annihilated* were systematically resorted to" by the papacy. That it could annihilate the faith of the people may well be doubted; but that it would be true to its instincts, spirit, and antecedents in stamping out the last vestige of legal organism and tactual descent may not well be doubted, at least until clearly disproven. That the traditions, the historic facts and practices, etc., of the primitive form of Christianity, found in the Culdee Church, brought much that was very valuable indeed to the Reformed Church of Scotland, and after which it patterned, there need be no doubt; but that to that body, and through it to its legitimate offspring, there was transmitted even presbyterially, to say nothing of prelatically, a tactual succession of ordinations from the apostolic age, does not appear in evidence, and must be left where transmissionism is always left, in the undemonstrated and evidently undemonstrable limbus of "obscurity" and conjecture.

Section VII.

IS THE DOCTRINE OF TRANSMISSION DEMONSTRABLE BY WAY OF ANY OTHER CLAIMANTS?

If other claimants there are to what is claimed by this doctrine, they find themselves inextricably involved in all the difficulties—indeed, impossibilities—of repudiating an authority and, at the same time, attempting to exercise legally and canonically functions of ministry in virtue of the authority thus renounced.

Section VIII.

VARIOUS OBJECTIONS TO APOSTOLICAL SUCCESSIONISM.

First. The origin, design, and qualifications of the apostolate render that office absolutely non-transferable from Peter or any other one of the apostles. The origin was by receiving their commission at the hands of the Lord Jesus personally (Luke vi, 13; Gal. i, 1), while his ministers are called by the mediation of the Holy Spirit. The design was not for authority or government, but to constitute a body of competent, intelligent men, who could bear reliable testimony to the life, teachings, sufferings, and resurrection of Christ. The qualifications, marks, or signs were to have been eye and ear witnesses of these things, either immediately as the eleven, or mediately or by evident consequence as Paul (Acts i, 21, 22); to be qualified by inspiration to announce doctrines to the Churches, and to enact laws which should carry with them the authority of God, and so be infallible guides to the Church, as the canon of Scripture was not yet complete (John vii, 13); to be endowed beyond others with the power of working miracles (Acts ii, 43; Heb. ii, 4), and being able to impart the gift to others by the imposition of their hands (Acts viii, 15-20); to be enabled to enforce their authority in the Churches by inflicting judgments on the disobedient (Acts v, 1-11; xiii, 8-11). To this fearful power Paul repeatedly alludes in his epistles. (2 Cor. xiii, 2; 1 Cor. iv, 21.)

While in the mere office of gospel ministers the apostles have left successors, every accepted minister of Jesus Christ (see chapter ii) being of the number; yet in all those things which went to distinguish them from other ministers, and confer on them a peculiarity and a superiority, they have left no successors. From the very nature of the case they could leave none. And if any, whether papist or Protestant, will pretend to be the successors of the apostles in their high and peculiar character, in that which distinguished them from ordinary ministers, then let them stand forth and show it—not merely claim it, but prove their succession by something more than mere words.

Second. The so-called argument from analogy, or that the same care which the Almighty One exercises over the preservation of the Holy Scriptures he will exercise over the ordaining and commissioning of men in a succession, once admitted (Ministerial Commission, p. 116), is inadequate, for such a succession is not "once admitted." If transmissionism can show such a record of preservation as can God's Word, let it stand forth and show it. Moreover, the argument is inconsistent, not discriminating between divine care of inanimate things and divine administration over the acts of voluntary agents, or persons; hence it has for its basis a fatalism which is destructive of all free agency, and which is utterly and forever inconsistent with the apostolic teachings as to moral responsible existence. The Lord would never construct an ecclesiastical system, we may safely say, for the maintenance of which he must force human wills. It would be wholly contrary to his method of government over moral agents.

Third. The claim that transmissionism is necessary to the unity of the Church is demonstrably false, because, what with Dominicans, Franciscans, Jacobites, Jansenists, Iconolatræ, etc., in the Papal Church; and High Church, Low Church, and Broad Church " altitude, platitude, and latitude," in Protestant prelatical succession Churches, personal successionism does not prevent sects. While in evangelical Protestantism there is a substantial unity, the unity of faith, it is not a religion of the senses, but of faith.

Fourth. *The doctrines involved in the claim.* There is, first, *sacerdotalism*—" priesthood "—with its concourse of ideas and spirit congenial to it; declaring its incumbents to be exclusively the successors of the apostles, and alone empowered to act as Christ's ambassadors, and that salvation is obtainable only within the pale of a prelatic Church. This is pleasing, of course, to its "clergy," because it invests them with a mysterious power and an awful sanctity, and gives them great importance in the eyes of their following, apart from moral character and mental ability—a principle which for so long kept the heathen oracles in credit; no wonder it sometimes culminates in priestly arrogance.

The whole idea, however, involved in this doctrine is contrary to the New Testament doctrine (Heb. ix, 25–28; x, 10–14), that Christ Jesus has made, by his oblation of himself *once* offered, a full, perfect, and sufficient sacrifice, oblation, and satisfaction for the sins of the whole world.

As the companion-piece to this doctrine, and subject to substantially the same objection, comes, second, *sacramentarianism*, which, exaggerating the value and force of the sacraments, teaches that, by some magic power transmitted by the succession, the officiating clergyman or priest is enabled to change the bread and wine in the Lord's Supper into the real body and blood of Christ—which is called the "real presence"—so that there is a saving virtue and efficacy in the mere reception of this sacrament; and that a mysterious virtue accompanies his act in baptism, so that regeneration is thereby obtained. Then, third, *ritualism*, which places an undue emphasis upon the observance of and dependence upon prescribed rites or forms in religion. The claim of transmissionism—successionism—being based upon the outward and visible, the whole system of worship accompanying it deals in the outward, the visible, the spectacular; hence, gorgeous ceremonies, elaborate rites, various vestments, candles, altars, bowings, and crossings; the outward rather than the inward, the ceremonial rather than the spiritual, become the prominent characteristic. Establish the doctrine of a specific mysterious virtue in the acts of some office-bearer, because of some particular mode of appointment to his office, and it is but a very short step to the doctrine that he imparts a special virtue to the sacraments, by which, independently of the mere temper of the recipient, they save his soul; then, a religion of forms without morals, transubstantiation, the adoration of the host, implicit reliance on the mediation of the priest, and numerous other delusions, follow in the train.

These doctrines, therefore, of transmission and successionism culminate inevitably in the principle that the Bible is not the sole authority in religion, only as it is explained and forced by the Church; and it is, therefore, utterly inconsistent with and absolutely antagonistic to a true Protestantism, which inheres in the right in all Christians to a practical protest against the authority of the Church when, by the teachings of its ministers or its own deliverances, it departs from the Bible or teaches contrary thereto. This right is based on the imperative and absolute duty of Christians to obey Christ as he has expressed himself in his Word. "The Bible, and the Bible alone, is the religion of Protestants." That, therefore, is irreconcilable with a true Protestantism and primitive Christianity which leads its adherents to assert as authority anything in opposition or in addition to the Holy Scriptures. Church Christianity the one, Bible Christianity the other. The moment the salvation of our fellow-men passes into the hands of a *"jure divino"* successional episcopacy, universally accepted, it can not fail to become a spiritual despotism. It creates an order of men with a distinct interest of its own, and with the means of ever successfully maintaining that interest, and so progressively attaining an absolute supremacy. It does not require a pope to produce the height of ecclesiastical despotism. Monarchy is no more despotic than oligarchy, and very likely to be less so. Against despotism, episcopacy, even an American episcopacy, denies the last resort allowable against secular despotism—*the right of revolution.* Bishop Cummins tried that resort, and with what result? Denunciation for perjury, deprivation of order, disowning by his Church; so that, unless the episcopal oligarchy be obeyed in all its towering innovations, schism and sect are the consequences; and schism and sect are then no longer schism and sect, but the true liberty of Christ against an antichrist sitting in the temple of God."*

Well did the learned and pious Dr. Doddridge say: "It is a very precarious and uncomfortable foundation for Christian hope which is laid in the doctrine of an uninterrupted succession of bishops, and which makes the validity of the ministrations of Christian ministers to depend upon such a succession."

Fifth. There is not one word, pro or con, in the Scriptures on the subject of an external transmission, or which in any way directly relates to it. The last three verses of the last chapter of Matthew are sometimes brought forward as if relating to the question in hand. They are the words of the Great Commission: "Go ye, therefore, and teach all nations," etc. From these words it is inferred, by those whom such inference will accommodate, that ordinations in the Church must invariably be confined to bishops, that the Church can not exist in the absence of such ordinations, and that no ministers are Christian ministers who are not thus ordained. But this is possibly only a case of party and sectarian prepossession; for so far as proving any of these things, it is not even remotely intimated in the passage that ordination at all is a Christian doc-

---

*Dr. Whedon, *Methodist Quarterly Review*, January, 1875; p. 120.

trine. With precisely equal propriety, and with no propriety at all, it might be argued that it proves that deacons must ordain, or that civil rulers must ordain. How can the text prove anything on a subject which is not in the remotest degree alluded to, or which is not in the passage supposed even to have been heard of? 2 Timothy ii, 2—"And the things that thou hast heard of me among many witnesses, the same commit thou to faithful men, who shall be able to teach others also"—is also relied upon in proof of a tactual succession. Unhappily, however, for these theorists, this text has no reference to the subject of the succession of ordinations contended for, as any one may see by consulting it, but speaks of a succession of instruction—"The things thou hast heard, . . . the *same* commit thou to faithful men," etc. Plainly, communication of instruction in gospel truth has nothing to do with successional ordination.

We are told that the instruction given by St. Paul to Timothy and Titus, concerning what they were respectively to do by way of supervision of the Churches in Ephesus and Crete, proves that Timothy and Titus were bishops. Suppose it does; what does that prove concerning an unbroken chain of ordinations—the so-called succession? Manifestly nothing. It might just as well be said that it proves some geographical proposition respecting the country of Palestine. There is no sort of relation between the premise and the conclusion that an uninterrupted succession of ordinations has been preserved.

But do the instructions of St. Paul to Timothy and Titus prove that they exercised episcopal functions? That they exercised supervisory authority and care over these newly formed Churches, and among these almost uninitiated Christians, we do not dispute, but cheerfully concede; nay, more, claim. But were they bishops of the modern order of prelates? If anything, the instruction of Paul proves, demonstrably, the very opposite. His letters were those of *command*, of authority, giving directions and exhortations as to what they were to do, and how they were to behave themselves as discreet and prudent ministers. (See 1 Tim. iii, 14, 15; iv, 14–16; v, 19–23; vi, 11–14, 20. 2 Tim. ii, 1, 2; iv, 1, 2, 21. Titus i, 5; ii, 1–7; iii, 9.) Is such language ever addressed to a bishop? Does a bishop thus *receive* the mandates of a superior? A bishop of the prelatical stamp is himself a prelate. He himself is the governor of ministers and Churches. He commands others. He does not himself receive instructions, such as we see all through the Epistles.

John xv, 15 and 16: "I have called you friends. . . . Ye have not chosen me, but I have chosen you, and ordained you," etc., is quoted; but it simply proves, what no one denies, that Christ ordained, in some manner, his own apostles. But there is not a hint as to a continuance of any chain of ordinations among men. Christ still does his own ordaining. A succession of manual impositions, being a dogma, requires specific proof, and yet we find no words of Scripture relating to such a proposition. Conscious of this, its advocates have endeavored to demonstrate its soundness and correctness chronologically, or in a way other than by the written Scriptures, which constitute the only source of information on the subject of the Christian ministry.

Sixth. There is no testimony presented by its advocates, as to the question of historic fact, that is relevant to the issue. Witnesses have been produced, of course, to prove the fact, but that is not necessarily the production of testimony. The witness may not know anything about the fact in question, although he may know many things about several other facts. So it is precisely with prelacy in the case in hand. Listen to the witnesses, and if any one of them says one word about, or in relation to, the fact of an apostolic succession of ordinations, then I have failed to hear him. Remember that the point in hand now is the fact of succession as distinguished from the doctrine of succession, which was examined in the immediately previous objection. The fact of succession is, of course, a historic question. It inquires into several historic facts. It inquires whether an apostle of Jesus Christ ordained a certain man, who ordained a certain other man, who ordained a certain other man, who ordained a certain other man, and so on down the catalogue of men's lives to the present day. Nothing but history can prove a historic question. Of course there is nothing in the Bible that can testify on this question, because the Bible was written before, or about, the time these alleged historic facts are supposed to have begun to occur. No testimony, therefore, can be relevant to the question before us but historic testimony.

Examining the witnesses which High-Churchism presents, and we have, as the first, *The Canons of the Church*. We are told that about the year 200 the Church of Rome passed the following canon, viz.: "Canon I. Let a bishop be ordained by two or three bishops."

Before this can be of much service, it must be shown whether the term "bishop" meant a ruler of pastors and Churches, a diocesan, or a pastor of a congregation. It is well known and admitted that in those days the word had most frequently the latter meaning. Also, whether this canon was actually enforced uniformly in all the Churches in the world, and continued to be so, and was never violated.

The doctrine of the succession is that it is a divine law; hence, if it be true that this canon was adopted by the Church at the time specified, then it completely destroys the doctrine of apostolic succession at a blow. Non-prelacy has maintained that bishops were set over presbyters and Churches as a mere human or Church regulation. The question has been whether the regulation was a divine regulation or a Church regulation. And this canon says that the Church adopted the law in the year 200, that bishops should ordain. This is all that we contend for, that the bishop is a bishop, and ordains by a mere Church law. Everybody knows that episcopacy has existed in the Church from a very early period. But the question has been whether it existed in pursuance of a divine or a human law; and we are informed by High-Churchmen themselves that episcopacy originated in a canon of the Church. It is hardly to be presumed that the Church would make a law requiring ordinations to be performed by bishops if it were already a well-known law of God. It does not avoid the difficulty to say, as is said, that this canon only prescribed the manner in which ordinations should be made; for it does not prescribe any manner;

it simply says that two or three bishops shall do the work. The canon is death to prelacy.

But what does the witness know about the question before us? It only tells us of what was required, but does not tell us what has been done, and that is the question being considered. It is very manifest that the law of the Church does not know any thing about the question in hand, does not pretend to know or to say a word, pro or con, in relation to it. In the very nature of the case it can not. A law is a rule, not a fact. History is fact, or a record of facts, and, of course, nothing can prove a fact of past existence but history. It is manifest that this witness does not pretend to know any thing about the question propounded, and must therefore be dismissed.

The next witness is *History*. Is it claimed by any man that history purports to prove a succession, an interrupted chain of ordinations, from the apostles to the present time? The only historic fact which was ever attempted to be produced by any writer on the apostolic succession is a list of bishops. These may be seen in any work on the subject, as Percival on "Apostolic Succession" and Chapin's "Primitive Church." Powell also quotes them; but nothing can be accomplished either way by their insertion here. The list most relied upon by High-Churchmen is a list of the names of the bishops, commencing with the Apostle John and ending with Bishop White, of the United States. We will not underrate these lists, whether claiming to come through the Sees of Rome or of Lyons. Is there one word said, or attempted to be said, implied or understood, by these lists on the subject of ordinations between Pothinus and Ætherius, in the See of Lyons, or between Augustine and Moore, in that of Canterbury—five hundred and ninety years in the one case, and eleven hundred years in the other? Not one word! These are only lists of incumbents in office.

But we are inquiring for a list of successive ordinations. A list of bishops who succeeded each other in office as incumbents is one thing, but a list of bishops who were the ordainers of one another is quite a different thing. Is it pretended by any, or claimed or imagined by any, that the bishops whose names stand in these lists were the ordainers of one another? that successive ordinations came down through them? Of course not. It is possible, confessedly, that in many instances the successor may have been ordained by his predecessor. That is, it is as likely, but no more so, if he was alive, that he was the ordainer, as any other bishop. The circumstance of his preceding him in office does not, by any means, increase the probability, but decreases it, that he was his ordainer, from the consideration that, in every instance, the *old bishop was dead before the new one came into office;* and the dead bishop could not ordain his successor.

These "lists," therefore, furnish us no information whatever on the subject of a succession of ordinations in the Church, even if admitting them to be correct history of that with which they purport to deal. The fact that no lists of *unbroken successive ordinations* is produced in evidence is proof conclusive that none exists; therefore this witness must be dismissed as knowing nothing of the matter at issue. Much ado is made over the testimony of the Christian writers who lived and wrote from the days of the apostles on to the fourth or fifth century, who are called, by way of honor or distinction, the Fathers. Such of their writings as are known to be genuine furnish excellent testimony as to historic facts belonging to the Church in their respective ages. Their opinions, of course, stand upon the same ground as the opinions of other men. Did space permit, I might insert quotations from Ignatius, Clement of Alexandria, Cyprian, Irenæus, and Jerome, which are considered the strongest and best in proving apostolic succession; and yet not a paragraph, sentence, or part of a sentence, pro or con, on the subject of a claim of successive ordinations in the Church, either for the preserving of the Church's being or for any other purpose, could be found in them. Their "invincible testimony" is found in the fact that those writers speak of *bishops* and of *presbyters* and of *deacons*, separately and distinctly. To me the striking feature is that every particle of this supposed testimony vanishes, so far as the question at issue is concerned, the moment it is considered that, whatever construction we give their language, or whatever we may suppose, imagine, or infer that they mean by the terms bishop, presbyter, and elder, they do not, in the slightest degree, intimate that this distinction arises from any divine command or arrangement. They simply and only speak of the distinction as *existing*. The very same distinction exists at the present day in many of the non-prelatical Churches. The question is not whether these distinctions, in the names or duties and prerogatives of ministers *existed* at any particular time, but whether they existed by virtue of divine command or as an arrangement of the Churches. Was this distinction the result of an inherently superior grade or order in the *office* of bishop itself, by command of Jesus Christ, or was it the result of an incidental or adventitious arrangement into which the Church voluntarily entered? A later discussion may show that the "bishop" of which the fathers speak was the pastor, and the "presbyter" was the same kind of minister, with this distinction only, that he was not being considered when thus named as the pastor of a Church, or as in the pastoral or supervisory relation.

It appears to have been taken for granted—a favorite method; from what logical premises or deductions it is certainly difficult to determine—that if it could be established that the Church at first had three orders in the ministry, the apostolical succession would follow of logical necessity. It is beyond the power of logic, and possibly beyond the power of history, to ascertain just how this idea ever obtained birth or currency. But so it is. It is quite certain that the apostolic succession, as held to lie in a line of bishops, can not be maintained without establishing the doctrine of three orders. But it is likewise quite as certain that the three orders may be established, and yet the doctrine of succession be left without a feather of support. Suppose the three orders were established, it still remains to be proven that it was the *permanent law* of the Church. Perhaps it would only prove that it would be best to have three orders in the ministry; that the Church would do better in that way; that it was necessary to the best results in the Church, but not to the being of a Church. To prove, if it could be proved, that at the first there were three orders in the ministry, either by divine or ecclesiastical law, proves, obviously, nothing conclusive on the subject of the apostolic succession; it only clears the way for, but does not take even the first step in, the discussion.

Now there is absolutely no more allusion in the writings of the Fathers to the notion of the successive chain of ordinations in bishops as a superior grade or order of ministers to elders or presbyters, in which or by virtue of which ordination is contained the vitality of the Church and the ministry, than is to be found in some treatise on navigation or agriculture. The subject is not hinted at. This witness, then, may be dismissed, as bearing no testimony relevant to the issue.

Seventh. This tactual succession theory makes Paul, the great apostle to the Gentiles, a *schismatic and wrong-doer.*

The doctrine is based on this wise: The only authority to preach and minister the gospel resided, in the first place, in Jesus Christ. After his death and resurrection, and a very short time before his ascension, he gave specific authority to his eleven apostles to preach, as recorded at the close of the Gospel by St. Matthew. Thus the only authority *in men* to preach resided in these eleven men personally. They had authority to preach and to communicate the authority to others, and they to others, and soon, by ordination personally performed, from man to man; and outside of this chain of successive ordinations there is no authority to preach.

This is the doctrine of successionism. He who presumes to preach outside of this chain of ordination is a schismatic and a wrong-doer.

Now, there is a twofold difficulty with regard to St. Paul. He was not one of these eleven men. He was a wicked sinner at the time, and for several years afterwards. But immediately on his becoming converted, without waiting for ordination, or for apostles, or for authority, he went forthwith to preaching. He preached several years, certainly, without the consent and without the knowledge of the apostles; for, according to the best and most probable history of his ministry, it was about four or five years after he commenced preaching that he went to Jerusalem, and the disciples would not recognize him as a minister or even as a disciple. (See Acts ix, 26, 27.) This was the first the apostles knew of him.

Here, then, was a schismatic and wrong-doer, as much as it is possible for any man to be schismatic and wrong-doer, according to the above doctrine. It is no argument at all to say that St. Paul was an apostle, and thus slur the matter over. The only authority on earth to preach the gospel resided in the eleven apostles, as first communicated to them; and supposing that they ordained

Matthias, then there were twelve. This is the root of all authority to preach. Paul certainly received no authority from them. But it may be said that Paul received his authority to preach directly from Christ, in virtue of his being an apostle. Then the foundation of the whole scheme is destroyed; because, in that event, the commission recited at the close of Matthew is not the only authority given by Christ to preach the gospel. And if Christ gave authority to one person outside the eleven, who can say how many or who else received authority in the same way? Some years after this, Paul was ordained at Antioch by "prophets and teachers," where it appears there was not an apostle present. Now, if no ministry is valid other than that which has its root in the commission which Christ gave to the eleven apostles as above, then Paul never did have authority to preach, for he was neither one of those eleven nor was he ordained by one of them.

But this is not the greatest difficulty. The apostolic succession is oftentimes attempted, or said to be attempted, to be traced *to him* as an original ordainer. But what is gained by tracing ordinations to him? The ordaining function was not in him; for he was not one of those on whom it was originally conferred, nor was he in the stream descending from them.

If St. Paul had original apostolic authority to

ordain, then he became possessed of it in some other way than by the commission given in the last of Matthew. And then that *other way*, whatever it be, is also a valid source from which to receive ordaining authority. Or, if the commission in Matthew be the original and only commission given to mankind—as is contended by High-Churchmen—then St. Paul is out of it; and had not only not authority to ordain others, but he had not even authority to preach himself." (Abbey.)

Eighth. There is no evidence that the successionism of prelacy is at all *necessary*. Physical contacts in ordination are plainly not needful for the transmission of sound doctrine and ethics. The physical can not thus touch and fashion that which is intellectual, moral, spiritual. Its most ardent advocates do not claim for it the virtue that it secures against the embracing and teaching of unsound and erroneous doctrine.

Ninth. This theory of apostolical succession, by way of an unbroken line of manual ordinations, is *essentially uncharitable in its spirit and bearing*, unchurching, as it does, the great mass of evangelical Christendom. Foremost in devoted usefulness in plucking sinners as brands from the eternal burning are the great denominations who reject that view of ministerial installation, toiling amidst Christ-like sacrifices in home and foreign fields, and gathering the fruitage into the garner of God; cultivating the Master's vineyard in all ways, spiritually, socially, intellectually, and bearing the heaviest burdens; and so blessed in it by the great Head of the Church, that in our land, and possibly in some others, they vastly preponderate among Christian workers in numbers and in religious, educational, and missionary exertions, and yet are declared, by the comparatively limited class of maintainers of this view to be destitute of the claims to true Churchliness, their sacraments unrecognized, and their large, intelligent, and pious ministry excluded, whenever possible, from the courtesies due to every ambassador of Christ. Of course it is said that numbers are no proof of truth, that a wrong cause may outnumber a good one. If quantity and numerical preponderance be the only possessions, the reply would be just. Paganism and popery have greater numerical strength than Protestant evangelical Christianity; and had they also equal or greater Scriptural piety and usefulness, then would the numerical argument be undeniably in their favor. The effect must have a cause adequate thereto. If the great bodies of Christians who dissent from this theory of prelatical succession have all the spiritual attributes of the true Church, and accomplish all its legitimate designs, not only equally with, but more extensively than, their prelatical neighbors, then certainly they may have, shall I say, a more valid claim to be considered true apostolic Churches. And it is not too much to say that the intolerance which brands them with ecclesiastical bastardy is an offense against high heaven as well as to the pious of earth. Nor is the offense other than shifted when it is said, as the author of "Vox Ecclesiæ" does say, p. 77: "The accusation against us, that we unchurch other bodies, makes us appear as most uncharitable; but, when examined closely, it means simply this: that we are not latitudinarian." Indeed! Then "other bodies" are "latitudinarian."

Tenth. Transmissionism carries with it the doctrine of the indelibility of Church orders, declaring that "once in orders, always in orders;" that a man once ordained can not voluntarily or by compulsion be severed from his commission, and return, or be returned, to the ranks of the laity; that only suspension of administering functions can be accepted or enforced. This places the Church where, while it must not, for the honor of God's cause, fail to excommunicate, it can not, after all, excommunicate, as has actually occurred in our own country in the case of one bishop found guilty of immorality, and of another who became a pervert to another faith—all this in violation of the Scriptural right of the

Church to apply holy discipline on the basis therefor in God's Word.

In concluding this chapter, to the man who says, "O well, the doctrine under discussion is only the doctrine of occasional individuals, but not of any Church," I would cite the words of Arthur W. Haddan, in his standard work on "Apostolic Succession in the Church of England," when he says (page 139): "The claim is written on the face of the solemn words of ordination in the Ordinal."

From very self-respect and consciousness of possession of the better way, we enter no complaint against "non-recognition canons," since true Churchliness does not depend upon the favor or disfavor of ecclesiastical regulations, born of human cunning rather than of divine commandment or apostolic precedent. But, proceeding to do the work given us to do by our own Master, we stand or fall.

Of course the historic facts, and "facts are stubborn things," and general principles, however unanswerable, adduced in this chapter, will have no force with a typical Romanist; for whatever tells for his Church is true, and whatever is adverse thereto is "a Protestant lie;" while Protestant transmissionists can dispose of all by sweetly and charmingly enforcing the before-mentioned "non-recognition canons."

In closing this chapter, I am ready to conclude with the learned Dr. Adam Clarke, in his comment on Ezekiel xxxiv, 23: "By the kind providence of God, it appears that he has not permitted any apostolic succession to be preserved, lest the members of the Church should seek that in uninterrupted succession which must be found in the Head alone. The papists, or Roman Catholics, who boast of an uninterrupted succession, which is a mere fable that never was and never can be proved, have raised up another head, the pope." Again he says: "Some make Heb. v, 4, an argument for the uninterrupted succession of popes and their bishops in the Church, who alone have authority to ordain for the sacerdotal office, and whosoever is not thus appointed is with them illegitimate. It is idle to employ time in proving that there is no such thing as an uninterrupted succession of this kind. It does not exist, it never did exist; it is a silly fable, invented by ecclesiastical tyrants, and supported by clerical coxcombs."

The vehemence with which transmissionism is maintained, and the virulence with which it is so often thrust upon our young constituency, must be the apology for the extended discussion which it has been given.

CHAPTER II.

DERIVATION, OR ACCREDITIZATION.

THIS is the doctrine that the visible Church is a divinely constituted organism—a covenanted compact of Christian believers, providentially associated for the ends and purposes of the Christian life; and that ministry in the Church is endowed with its functions by "the call of God," and *derives* its legal status for the exercise of its prerogatives "by the authority of the Church," the body of believers; recognizing "the call" as manifested by "gifts, grace, and usefulness," and approbating and accrediting in the name of the Lord Jesus, the Head of the Church and the sole source of all authority in his kingdom.

As to the correctness of this formula let the facts which follow attest.

Section I.

THE TERM CHURCH DEFINED.

Inasmuch as the Bible is not a book of specific rules and definitions, but of principles; and since there is no single, simple, and concise definition in the apostolic or other Scripture writings of the institution called "Church," our definition must be gathered from the use of the word in the various passages and their contexts where it is employed.

From the New Testament Greek the word *Ekklesia* is translated "Church," and is used as the correspondent term to *quohal*, *yedah*, and *miquera*, in the Hebrew Scriptures. In both languages these words are derived from words signifying to convoke, to call out or call together, to assemble; hence, the primary meaning is an assembly or congregation, whether organized or mobocratic; *e. g.*, Acts xix, 32 and 39, the word *ekklesia* is used for an "assembly"—whether "confused" as in the former, or "lawful" as in the latter. The word in its civil use in the purely democratic States was applied to the assemblies of the people, persons possessing common privileges, who were called out by the public herald into some certain place, to deliberate together on common interests, and to transact the business of the community. Slaves, foreigners, and criminals could form no part of such a congregation, or *ekklesia*. In like manner Christ's *Church* is, first, a community of free men. There are no slaves in it, and no criminals; no strangers, or foreigners. It is, second, a community gathered together for a public purpose. It has been, third, gathered together by a *call*. It is divinely *called out* from among the mass of those who are determined to be slaves or criminals, or who are willfully willing to remain foreigners and strangers to Christ and Christianity.

There are several different but closely allied meanings in the Scriptures of the word Church. The most exalted and comprehensive is,

First: The *Church Catholic and Invisible*, which embraces all who have been and all who shall be united to Christ—"the whole number of the elect," if you please—whether in heaven or on earth. This is the culmination of the idea of the Church—this, the holy city, New Jerusalem, coming down from God out of heaven, "prepared as a bride adorned for her husband."

Paul, in his charge to the Hebrews to follow peace with all men, advance in holiness of life, and guard against contentions, enforces his exhortation by the obligations arising from their relation to this invisible and universal Church. He says (Heb. xii, 22, 23): "But ye are come unto Mount Zion and unto the city of the living God, the heavenly Jerusalem, and to an innumerable company of angels, to the general assembly and Church of the first-born which are written in heaven, and to God, the Judge of all, and to the spirits of just men made perfect."

These Hebrew Christians, by virtue of their faith, enjoyed communion with God, and while yet upon earth sustained the same relations to him as did the departed worthies; they were enrolled citizens of Mount Zion, the heavenly Jerusalem, and members of the general assembly and Church of the first-begotten of God, whose names are written in heaven's Church-record. They are children, free-born, of Jerusalem which is above, which is the mother of the redeemed, and truly free children of the Eternal Father. Wherefore, says the same apostle to the Ephesians (ii, 19-22): "Now, therefore, ye are no more strangers and foreigners, but fellow-citizens with the saints, and of the household of God; and are built upon the foundation of the apostles and prophets, Jesus Christ himself being the chief corner-stone; in whom all the building, fitly framed together, groweth unto a holy temple in the Lord; in whom ye also are builded together for a habitation of God through the Spirit." The first chapter of Ephesians is replete with the thought of the spiritual body. The apostle therein declares it to be God's eternal conception and purpose to unite into one spiritual body all who have been or shall be born from above; his fixed design that, in the dispensation of time, "he might gather *together in one* all things in Christ, both which are in heaven and which are on the earth, even in him. . . . And hath put all things under his feet, and gave him to be the head over all things to the Church, which is his body, the *fullness* of him that filleth all in all." "He is the head of the body, the Church." In Ephesians v, 25-31, we have the annunciation of the spiritual nuptials of the unseen Christ and his invisible bride: "Husbands, love your wives, even as Christ also loved the Church [his spouse] and gave himself for it, that he might sanctify and cleanse it with the washing of water, by the word; that he might present it to himself a glorious Church, not having spot or wrinkle or any such thing, but that it should be holy and without blemish." Verse 29 declares it to be no fanciful union, but a real relation: "For no man ever yet hated his own flesh, but nourisheth and cherisheth it, even as the Lord the Church." The spiritual basis of this union and its correspondent relations are found in the fact that we are in him and of him. "For we are members of his body, of his flesh, and of his bones." As Eve was formed from the man, and united to him, so each believer, and the grand aggregate of all believers—the Church unseen—is derived from the second Adam, "the Lord from heaven," and is indissolubly united to him in an eternal marriage. "And they two shall be one flesh." To guard against all error in the application of what he has said, the apostle adds: "This is a great mystery; but I speak concerning Christ and his Church." All this is referable only to the spiritual body of Christ—the invisible Church—which was inaugurated when the venerable fathers of the race exercised faith in the promised "seed of the woman," and which is to terminate in the inheritance incorruptible. It is language which can be applied only to the spiritual, unseen, and catholic Church. Her abiding city, the provisions for her festal hours, her magnificent temple for worship, and freedom from contact with all impurity, are certainly inapplicable to any visible organization. If it be said, This is the Church triumphant, I reply, Whether militant or triumphant, it is the Church *invisible*, seen only "in the spirit." It is the Church *catholic*, for "the nations of them that are saved shall walk in the light of it." (Rev. xxi, 24.) It is the virgin bride of the Lamb (Rev. xxi, 9)—his chaste spouse (Song of Solomon iv, 7); therefore, *indefectible*, ay, *indestructible;* hence, "the gates of hell shall not prevail against it." (Matt. xvi, 18.) "Of this gospel Church,* in its highest and most comprehensive meaning, our Lord Jesus Christ is declared to be the Head—the source of life to each member of his body—the Chief Shepherd of this flock and fold. But while all true Christians are thus united to him and have in him a

---

* "The Ecclesiastical Polity of the New Testament," by G. A. Jacobs, D. D., of the Church of England; p. 11.

common life, the Church, in this sense, being at present altogether a spiritual body, has no visible form or organization in the regulation of which man has anything to do, however instrumentality may be employed in bringing men, one after another, into it. The place and time of its manifestation in its completeness as an organized community, or what St. Paul terms a *politeuma*, is not on earth or in the existing gospel dispensation." The invisible unity of the Church magnifies Christ and demonstrates brotherhood in him.

Second. *The Church Catholic and Visible. Catholic:* This word in the early creeds, as in its primary signification, had a good meaning, denoting the one universal body, as opposed to fragmentary and isolated heresies and schisms, which were separations from the true Church. Those who contend for its application to visible unity throughout the world, under one visible head, are not only confronted by the falling asunder of Eastern and Western Christendom, but by the language of the apostles as well; who, while they teach that there is but one Church composed of believers throughout the world, think it not at all inconsistent with this to speak of "the Churches of Judea," "the Churches of Galatia," "the seven Churches which are in Asia," and "the Church of Ephesus." These apostles had among themselves no common head, but planted Churches and gave directions for their government, in most cases, without any apparent correspondence with each other; and yet, in connection with this, hear the words of Paul (1 Cor. xii, 12, 13): "For as the body is *one*, and hath many members, and all the members of that one body, being many, are one body, so also is Christ. For by one Spirit are we all baptized into one body, whether we be Jews or Gentiles, whether we be bond or free; and have been all made to drink into one Spirit." And, again, in the salutation to the Church at Corinth, he says (1 Cor. i, 2): "Unto the Church of God which is at Corinth, to them who are sanctified in Christ Jesus, called to be saints *with all* that in *every* place call upon the name of Jesus Christ our Lord, both theirs and ours." From all which we are led to conclude that the visible Church consists of all those who throughout the world profess their faith in the Lord Jesus Christ; it therefore comprehends various bodies of believers, differing from each other in some particulars, but united in acknowledging the Scriptures of the Old and New Testament as the only and sufficient rule of faith and practice, and Jesus Christ as the sole Head of the Church, and conformably observe the ordinances of the Gospel.

Visible. Not that there are two Churches—the one visible, and the other invisible; but the former is the natural and inevitable product, the logical sequence of the latter; its sensible and recognized representative, including that part of the invisible which is still on earth, and denoting all who make a credible public profession of its faith; its assemblies, and several parts and acts of worship, being observed by all men. In harmony with this idea is Paul's utterance: 1 Cor. i, 2; xii, 12, 13.

Visibility includes—

(*1.*) *The Church Local.* This is the most simple and primary use of the word in the New Testament. The name *ekklesia* (Church) is applied to persons, whether many or few, who are united in some certain place or locality for the worship of God and his Christ; thus Acts xiv, 23: "And when they had ordained them elders in every *Church*, and had prayed with fasting, they commended them to the Lord, on whom they believed." The word is applied to the Church in some certain place or locality, thus: "The Church that was at Antioch" (Acts xiii, 1); "And when they were come and had gathered the Church together," etc. (Acts xiv, 27); "As I teach everywhere in every Church" (1 Cor. iv, 17); "If, therefore, the whole Church be come together into one place" (1 Cor. xiv, 23); "And when he had landed at Cesarea, and gone up and saluted the Church" (Acts xviii, 22). Usually, when the Christians of a country or nation are spoken of collectively, the word is always in the plural number, as "the Churches of Galatia," "the Churches of Judea," etc. Persons associated together by profession, and for the worship of Christ in private houses, have the name *ekklesia* (Church) applied to them: "Greet Priscilla and Aquila, my helpers in Christ Jesus; likewise greet the Church that is in their house" (Rom. xvi, 3–5); "Aquila and Priscilla salute you much in the Lord, with the Church that is in their house" (1 Cor. xvi, 19); "Salute Nymphas, and the Church which is in his house" (Col. iv, 15); "To the Church in thy house, grace and peace from God, our Father, and from the Lord Jesus Christ" (Philemon, 3). Whether in the latter class of texts the word Church implies only the persons named and their children and servants; or, in addition to these, other persons who, professing the faith, repaired to their houses at stated times to hear the Word and to unite in the exercises of prayer and praise—encouraged by the gracious promise of our Savior that "where two or three are gathered together in my name, there am I in the midst of them"—is quite immaterial; in either event, the apostle says it was a *Church*.

This New Testament and apostolic use of the word harmonizes with the Old Testament Scriptures. Although the English word Church does not occur in the authorized version, yet the Greek word *ekklesia*, which is rendered *Church* in the New Testament is of frequent occurrence in the Greek, called the Septuagint, version of the Old Testament, and is there translated as *congregation*. Take, as a striking example, Psalm xxii, 22: "I will declare thy name unto my brethren: in the midst of the *congregation* will I praise thee." Here the word *ekklesia* is translated *congregation*. In Heb. ii, 12, Paul quotes the Psalmist: "I will declare thy name unto my brethren; in the midst of the *Church* will I sing praise unto thee." Here the word *ekklesia* is translated church. The *congregation* of the Psalmist is the *Church* of the apostle. The latter says: "Unto the Church of God, to them that are sanctified in Christ Jesus, called to be saints, with all that in every place call upon the name of Jesus Christ our Lord, both theirs and ours." (1 Cor. i, 2. See also Eph. i, 22; also ii, 19-22; iii, 15; iv, 11, 12; v, 27; Gal. i, 2, 22, etc.)

To the generic idea of *ekklesia*, assembly, add the idea of a religious purpose, and to this the idea of organization for that religious purpose, and we have an assembly organized for a religious purpose, which implies a government, with officers for its administration and the actual performance of the acts for which the government was organized, as a definition of a Church. In short, it is but little more than the plural of

Christian; it is Christians in association *as such*. Any number of believers in the Lord Jesus Christ, in covenanted compact on Gospel principles for the maintenance of Christian fellowship and worship in all things pertaining thereto, constitute a Christian Church.

That it may appear that this view is also historically correct, we continue to quote from a previous citation—from Mosheim's Church History: "In those primitive times each Christian Church was composed of the people, presiding officers, and the assistants, or deacons. These must be the component parts of every society. The principal voice was that of the people, or of the whole body of Christians; for even the apostles themselves inculcated, by their example, that nothing of any moment was to be done or determined on but with the knowledge and consent of the brotherhood (Acts i, 15; vi, 3; xv, 4; xxi, 22); and this mode of proceeding both prudence and necessity required in those early times. The assembled people, therefore, elected their own rulers and teachers, *or, by their free consent, received such as were nominated to them.* [Italics the essayist's.] They also, by their suffrages, rejected or confirmed the laws that were proposed by their rulers in their assemblies; they excluded profligate and lapsed brethren, and restored them; they decided the controversies and disputes that arose; they heard and determined the causes of presbyters and deacons; in a word, the people did everything that is proper for those in whom the *supreme power* of the community is vested."

However, the Churches founded by the apostles, while maintaining their local autonomy, were not the same as in modern times are called Independent, which claim that every particular society of visible professors, agreeing to walk together in the faith and order of the Gospel, is a complete Church; that the whole power of government is vested in the *cœtus fidelium, the assembly of the faithful,* for the reason that during the life of the apostles and evangelists those Churches were subject to their counsel and control. Therefore, the independency of separate societies was not the first form of the Church.

It may be allowed that possibly some of the smaller and more insulated Churches did, after the death of those men, retain that form for a time; but the large Churches in the chief cities, and those planted in populous neighborhoods, had many presbyters or elders; and as the members multiplied they had several separate assemblies, or congregations, yet all under the same government. This will appear more fully as we note—

(2.) *The Church Federative*—league, connectionalism, compact, or solidarity. This use of the word harmonizes with the former, inasmuch as the autonomy of the Church local is maintained, the federative principle being the embodiment in the entity as a whole of all matters pertaining to the common weal, and the retention by local and particular bodies of such matters as do not so pertain.

That such use of the word was made will appear if we will recall the previous citation, how that the children of Israel, numbering many thousands, and with tribal divisions, and later with the synagogue system, are spoken of in their collective capacity as a congregation, and the term used interchangeably with the word Church in the New Testament.

Then the Church of Palestine comprehended a large number of Churches in associated compact (Acts ix, 31): "So the Church throughout all Judea and Galilee and Samaria had peace," etc. (Revised Version.) The Churches of a city are never spoken of in the apostolic writings but the Church, notwithstanding that, in many of the large cities, before church edifices were constructed sufficient to accommodate the multitudes of believers in the place, there must have been many small congregations, with their elders, or pastors, which were under one common government, *e. g.*: "Now there were in the Church that was at Antioch certain prophets and teachers" (Acts xiii, 1); "And the hand of the Lord was with them, and a great number believed and returned unto the Lord" (Acts xi, 21); "And it came to pass that a whole year Saul and Barnabas assembled themselves with the Church and taught much people; and the disciples were first called Christians at Antioch." (Acts xi, 26.) There were very many converts before the year's successful work of Saul and Barnabas; hence should have been called "a great number" and "much people" if they were but one congregation convened in one house. The same is true of Ephesus and other cities; yet we read only of the Church of those cities, and not congregations; therefore the connectional or federative character of the Church is irresistibly inferable. In the case of the most ancient Church of them all, that of the metropolis of Palestine, the Church in Jerusalem, we have ample data on this point. Thus on the day of Pentecost "three thousand souls were added to the Church." Shortly after this it was recorded: "And the Lord added *daily* to the Church such as should be saved." In Acts iv we find another numerical statement: "Howbeit many of them who heard the word believed; and the number of men [exclusive of women] was about five thousand." In chapter v it is further stated: "And believers were the more added to the Lord, multitudes both of men and women." Twenty or so years later, they said to

Paul when in Jerusalem: "Thou seest, brother, how many thousands of Jews there are that believe." The original, it seems, is, literally, *how many tens of thousands;* that is a vast multitude. For these many congregations places of assembling are needed. But, being united under one form of government, it is still called *ekklesia*, the Church, and not *Churches, e. g.:* "And great fear came upon all the *Church.*" (Acts v, 11.) "And at that time there was a great persecution against the Church which was at Jerusalem." "As for Saul, he made havoc of *the Church,* entering into every house, and haling men and women, committed them to prison." (Acts viii, 1–3.) "Then tidings of these things came unto the ears of the Church which was at Jerusalem." (Acts xi, 22.) That there were more assemblies than one in that city is evident, not only from the number of converts specified in the Acts, many of whom might be strangers, and afterward removed to other places, and from the fact that the apostles continued a long time in it after the day of Pentecost—not all, surely, to minister to a single society of believers—but also from the fact that the poor were so numerous that not one deacon, but seven, were appointed to take care of them. The New Testament principle requires, as far as possible, the unity of all the faithful; and the same principle of Christian brotherhood which prompts a number of individuals to meet together for religious fellowship, inevitably leads to a broader unification.

(*3.*) *The Church Representative.* In the unified body, doctrines must be formulated, usages must be defined, difficulties authoritatively adjusted, the common defense provided for, and aggressive movements harmoniously concerted. It was found to be impracticable for the several congregations to assemble in one democratic body for this purpose, and even if practicable, undesirable and useless; hence, it appears that a representative body was constituted whose admonitions and counsels were authoritative, and whose decisions were binding. A case in point (Acts xv) is that of the Church at Antioch, where a grave question had arisen that threatened to disturb the peace of the Church. Certain men were chosen to go up to Jerusalem and refer the matter to the apostles and elders. When they had arrived, it is said, "The apostles and elders came together to consider of this matter." "And the day following, Paul went in with us unto James, and all the elders were present." The elders of the congregation in Jerusalem, with James as their presiding officer, are in solemn session, by special appointment, to consider the question sent up by the Church at Antioch, and to give a deliverance thereon for the future guidance of the Churches, which, "with the whole Church" (verse 22), they did. This was manifestly a representative body—the first ecclesiastical General Conference mentioned in the annals of the Church. "In the history of the Christian Church, the councils form centers of development with respect to doctrine, liturgy, and constitution. They grew up from the very needs of the Church, and in the Apostolic Council at Jerusalem (reported in Acts xv) they found their model and their legitimation." (Schaff-Herzog "Enc. of Religious Knowledge.")

The constitution of the Church is found in Holy Writ—it is organic, fundamental. Statutory enactments under it are particular, prudential, and applicatory. The latter must be in strict subordination to and in conformity with the former.

The venerable formula—"The visible Church of Christ is a congregation of faithful men, in which the pure Word of God is preached and the sacraments duly administered according to Christ's ordinance, in all those things that of necessity are requisite to the same"—can be cordially received as a fair summary. The expression, "The visible Church of Christ," is a declaration indirectly of the Church catholic and invisible, and directly of the Church catholic and visible, but does not involve the absolute uniformity and unity in all details of that visibility. The evils of sectarianism are to be deplored, but that ism is more a thing of the spirit than of any diversity in organisms. Intellectual unity is not possible among uneven minds, and the impossible is not obligatory; a mere external apparent unity of profession and name—temporary discipline and symbolism, without a co-ordinate intellectual unity delighting to express itself through that form, would be an intolerable burden. Yet oneness in the great cardinal doctrines of evangelical truth is not only possible, but is realized. Those who perpetually ring changes on "Union," "Union," are quite invariably found, in the final issue, to mean union with their particular sect; while those who say, "No Christian union without ecclesiastical unity," raise the suspicion that they fulminate in the interests of their particular ecclesiasticism.

The phrase, "*is a congregation of faithful men,*" plainly uses the word "congregation" in a comprehensive sense, including the Church local and the Church federative; the associative principle being as proper and binding in the one case as in the other. That it must be a congregation of "faithful men" indicates that a constitutional Church principle is that of *fellowship on the basis of the Christian faith*, not fellowship founded on an official figment. "The kingdom of God is not meat and drink, but righteousness, and peace, and joy in the Holy Ghost." "I am well aware that the context in which this passage is imbedded, like a diamond in its setting, clearly shows that it relates to an individual, and not to a corporate Christianity. It refers to a kingdom whose subjects are all the faculties and characteristics and qualities of the heart. It suggests the picture of our King enthroned in the bosom of a sinner saved by grace. But, after all, what is the true Church of God? . . . Is it not the aggregation of these spiritual units? The tiniest petal of a fern-leaf is a miniature of the whole. A crystal spar is made up of smaller crystals, every one of which is the perfect image (even with microscopic scrutiny) of that which it helps to compose. So perfect is the resemblance between the saved believer and the spiritual Church that the one is a microcosm of the other. Hence, what St. Paul here affirms of the individual child of God, is equally a representation of the blessed *company* of all faithful people. The essential characteristics of the true Church are a spotless righteousness, a perfect peace with God, and a joy of which the world knows nothing." (Bishop Cheney.)

It is the evident design of the Head of the Church to bring believers in the Lord Jesus Christ into organization in order to separate and distinguish them from the world, thus enabling them the better to cultivate and exemplify the principles of righteousness; therefore, those who profess godliness and speak lightly of the Church, and say, just as do the ungodly, that they can serve God as well out of it as in it, evidently forget, or intentionally overlook, the fact that all the religious light they have received has come to them through the Church, and that God's Church is the only agency that is doing anything worthy of notice toward ameliorating the condition of mankind. It is as true now as in the days of Christ that the Church is "the light of the world"—"the salt of the earth;" therefore, it should be spoken of only in terms of the highest respect. And they who are endeavoring to do the will of the Lord outside of the Church, are as truly out of their proper place as they who, being in it as its members, are not trying earnestly to do that will. Involved in this covenanted compact of "faithful men" is the principle of *the application of holy discipline* on the rules therefor in God's Holy Word. (Matt. xviii, 15–20, etc.) Hear the Church!

Reversing, for temporary convenience, the two remaining clauses, we have next "*the sacraments duly administered*" as a requisite constitutional Church principle; while that "*the pure Word of God is preached*" is another. No body of persons can constitute a Scriptural Church without it. Even an "apostolical succession" of technical ecclesiasticism, without it, could not meet the requirement; while an *evangelical succession* of faith and doctrine could, and, the Lord be thanked, does. Indeed, the only apostolical succession that is worth anything is the succession of apostolical truth—of the Gospel—as apostolical men proclaimed it. That is necessary, and, fortunately, that does not depend on the hands through which it has been transmitted to us. The truth of the Epistle to the Romans, for example, does not depend on whether we received it through a thousand hands from Rome or five thousand hands from Corinth, so that we have the genuine epistle, any more than the nutritive properties of a loaf of bread depend on our ability to trace it through a baker, miller, merchant, farmer, etc., to the harvest-field. If it be bread, it is not the less nutritive because we do not know the pedigree of its transmission. If the Bible be conceded to be the inspired truth of God, it is not the less true because we can not trace the hands through which it passed from the pen that first traced its pages. As all parties, here in question, concede that we have the genuine apostolical teaching in the New Testament, we have only to go to that and drink from the fountain itself, and not depend on a long and tortuous pipe, that may be alleged to run through the centuries of corruption and darkness, for the blessed water of life. This is what Jesus and the apostles have told us to do, and we are satisfied with their authority.

If the pure Word of God be preached and the sacraments duly administered, there must be a class or order of ministry with preaching and administering functions.

Section II.

HOW IS MINISTRY SCRIPTURALLY CONSTITUTED?

The answer to this inquiry must consist of deductions from Scripture facts or precedents, as quoted in the preceding section, from which it appears plain that there are three parties to the ministerial office; namely, the Lord Jesus Christ, the minister himself, and the Church. In order to investiture with this office, practically, properly, validly, there must be the recognition of both the other parties to the contract; namely, the Master who "calls" and "sends" him, and the Church for which he ministers. The latter is not a party to the "call" to the ministry beyond the recognition of it, where it exists, by the signs—"gifts, grace, and usefulness." If the candidate have not this "divine call" (that is, the inward impression and conviction by the Holy Ghost of the duty of performing that work and impulsion towards it) he is surely no minister of Christ to the Church. If the Church do not in some way, by some public and authoritative mode, give her approbation, he is certainly not an accredited minister to men. While the fact of the "call" makes it his duty to preach, the fact of necessitated authorization makes it his duty only upon condition that the Church, by recognition of the appropriate signs, can be induced to come into the arrangement. Herein, then, lies the importance, the necessity, of some suitable induction into office—of ordination. The Lord Jesus, infinitely capable of attending to his own affairs, does not relegate them to men—he has no vicegerency on earth—and hence, by the Holy Spirit, himself "calls" men personally to this work. Thus, while the work of the ministry is initially between Christ and the minister, ordination is between the Church and the minister. Philosophically considered, the principle of agency or ministry is the same in religion as in the other affairs of life. A minister is *sent* from his principal—government or personage—on an errand to communicate something to some other government or personage. How, then, can he be a minister of the gospel who is not *sent* by the Lord Jesus to minister his will to the people? This doctrine is Scriptural. Paul tells us (Eph. iv, 11) that God "gave" the various ministries or ministers; and in Hebrews (v, 4) he records the significant declaration: "No man taketh this honor unto himself, but he that is called of God, as was Aaron." This is referred to as being, in some important sense, the type of that of all true gospel ministers. We note three points of interest:

(1.) Aaron received a call directly from God to go into the wilderness and meet Moses, and undertake whatever duties that interview might disclose. (Exodus iv, 27.) (2.) Aaron received an indirect call from God by the hand of one to whom God had also made known his will concerning him; namely, Moses. (Exodus iv, 14.) (3.) Aaron was inducted into his office with certain solemn formalities, whereby his mind must have been still more strongly impressed with the importance of his sacred duties which he was thenceforth to perform, and all Israel was made to know that God had chosen him to minister at the altar. (Lev. viii.) Hence, to be "called of God as was Aaron" implies a direct divine call to the ministry—something above human authority, something without which all human authority is nothing and worse than nothing. Thus Paul declares himself to be "an apostle, not of men, neither by man, but by Jesus Christ and God the Father." (Gal. i, 1.) He thanked "Jesus Christ, our Lord" for "putting him into the ministry." (1 Tim. i, 12.) Thus he felt that a dispensation of the gospel was committed to him, and he was constrained to exclaim, "Necessity is laid upon me; yea, woe is unto me if I preach not the gospel." (1 Cor. ix, 16.) Of course we are not now authorized, indeed, to expect such visions and revelations as were vouchsafed Paul; nevertheless, a divine hand must open the door, and a divine voice must invite him to enter, who is a true minister of the Lord Jesus Christ. Whenever a man is truly called to enter the ministry the Church will know it. When the Lord calls a man to preach he calls others to hear him. The call of the individual to the ministry implies the call of the Christian body to be a Church. Ever since the organization of the Church it has been its solemn duty to recognize and lead forward to the work such as, in its godly judgment, are designated for it, and to warn aside any who may be ready to run before they are sent.

In such view incumbents of the ministerial office are seen to be only one of the constituent parts of the Church, and not the Church itself. The laity are not members of the ministry, but of the Church, while ministers are but members of, and officers in, the Church. The action of the Church in recognizing the divine call, and sending the minister forth properly accredited as duly qualified, is the essence of ordination, its end and seal. Hence it is the *Church* that ordains. An advocate of the doctrine of transmission of priestly or ministerial authority by a succession of commissions, the author of "Vox Ecclesiæ," says: "The doctrine of succession is based upon the principle that man can not originate a Church; that is Christ's prerogative. Man can not, therefore, qualify his fellow-man to act as a minister in Christ's Church. No one can give to another what he does not possess; therefore no layman, or number of laymen, can, by any possibility, give authority to minister in the word and sacraments, for the simple reason that they themselves have not that authority. Each and every clergyman, then, must receive his commission from at least one who is already in the ministry; *he,* in turn, from others holding the same great office, and so on back from generation to generation until we reach those to whom Christ said: 'As my Father hath sent me, even so send I you. Go ye therefore into all the world, and preach the gospel to every creature, and lo, I am with you alway, even unto the end of the world.' To all who are duly ordained, then, in this succession belong the special promise of the Lord, the right to preach his gospel, administer his sacraments, and exercise discipline in his Church; and these rights, or powers, belong to no person whatever who is not so ordained. However pious, zealous, eloquent, or learned a man may be, if he has not been regularly called and sent into the Lord's vineyard by those having lawful authority, he is not truly a minister of Christ."

This is, to say the least, a strong putting of

his doctrine. A no less strong putting of the doctrine that ministerial authority is *derived* and not transmitted, is that of Henkle, in "Analysis of Principles of Church Government," thus: "An ambassador can not create an ambassador, this being the work of the supreme power. He may judge of qualifications, acknowledge claims to genuineness, and indorse them to others; but the authority, to be really valid, must come from him alone, whether king or president, who may enjoy the supreme authority. Thus Christ instituted the ministry, and decreed its perpetuity in a succession of faithful men of apostolic zeal and purity; but while he left to them the management of much that respects economic details, he held distinctly in his own hands this great matter of succession, by reserving the sole power of creating his own ambassadors, to the end of the line. Mark the terms of the commission: 'Go preach my gospel,' etc., and 'lo, I am *with* you to the *end of the world.*' Those to whom this was first spoken were only to live and labor for a few years, and how could he be *with* them in their ministrations to the *end* of the *world?* Thus, 'I *am* now with *you;* and when you pass off the stage, and the future becomes the present, my word is still heard by those I shall call to succeed you; I am with *you,*' and so on, to the final end. It would be strange if the supreme authority—the king, if you please—should commit the whole appointing power of officers for a long expedition to a subordinate officer, when the king declared, on making the first appointment, that he should himself be *with the expedition* all the time to the end. . . . Christ, then, ordained and published in the original commission that there should be a perpetual succession of ministers in the Church and the world; and, effectually to secure this end, he decreed that he would own no man-made minister, but only such as were called by himself. But as these were designed to act in harmony with each other and co-operatively with the Church, it was fit that they should be suitably accredited to each other, to the Church, and to the world. Here there are given various marks and indications by which a man is to judge whether the inward movings on his spirit are of the Holy Ghost, and by which also his brethren may form a tolerably reliable judgment on the same question. When those marks and indices are found, and his own inward convictions corroborate them, the proper authorities of the Church may, with a good degree of safety, admit him to a state of trial in the ministry, where he will be able, by the further evidence of fruit-bearing, to satisfy both them and himself that he is truly called of God to the sacred work. Should the evidence of fruit of his labor appear, he may then be admitted as a true minister of Christ, by such appropriate ceremony as the Church may deem it proper to employ, and thus accredit his claims to the Church and the world.

In all, however, that is done in the premises by the existent ministry and the Church, nothing more is legitimately intended than to declare, formally and officially: "We believe, from all the evidence and after due trial, that God has called this man to be a minister of his Word, and we accordingly acknowledge him in that character." This is the true succession, and this is all that the Church and the ministry have to do in perpetuating it. And does it seem reasonable that one called of God to the work should be denied recognition, unless his claims be indorsed by the action of some particular individual pursuant to his own sweet will? Can the Lord Jesus be thus utterly dependent on an erring mortal for a valid succession of the ministers of his grace?"

In our American Republic all public officers, from the President to the "pathmaster," are in some way installed, inducted, inaugurated—ordained, if you please—according to such methods as Congress and the Legislatures may direct. But that, abstractly and specifically considered, does not give them the right to their office. The oath of office, received at the hands of the chief-justice, is not that which makes some particular man

President of the Union; for if so, then the same chief-justice could make any other man President to whom he might administer the same oath. When the chief-justice rightfully administers the oath, which is the act of ordination, he acts, not on his own behalf by prerogative, but simply as the executive, in that matter, of the will of the Nation. In this case it is the Nation that ordains.

The beginning of ecclesiastical power is illustrated by the first ecclesiastical meeting after the ascension of Christ, as recorded in Acts i, 15–26, in which the whole "hundred and twenty"— probably the entire number of disciples of Christ in and about Jerusalem—participated. Then, also, in the election of the seven. (Acts vi, 1–7.) The aggregate body assembled, the Church and the apostles both acting their part. And, again, the procedure recorded in Acts xiii, 1–3, while not describing, perhaps, an *ordination* in the common usage of the words, yet, with the foregoing, indicates how authority is *derived* from the body of believers. Hence, *it is the Church that ordains.* However, while through its constituted method, whether aggregated or delegated, the Church may designate upon whom it will confer authority to act in a ministerial capacity, and may act legislatively and judicially, yet it can not conveniently, indeed, not possibly, act executively; therefore, it must have a constituted agent, representative, or executive officer, who, not by inherent prerogative, but "by the authority of the Church," shall perform the interesting, significant, and important ordinative act for it. *It is the Church that ordains.*

It will be said that this leads logically to lay ordination, or the legitimacy of an ordaining act by lay members, but this is just what it does not do; it leads to *Church* ordination. No layman could act legitimately save by the action or order of the covenanted compact, the corporate body, the Church; then he would not be acting as a layman at all, but as the representative or servant of the body, acting *ministerially for* and *in behalf of* the Church, the associative body. Christ's words concerning his Church being true—"The gates of hell [death] shall not prevail against it"—it is safe to say that if in the progress of the work a body of believers should arise in some remote island of the sea; or if, in the emergencies and exigencies of human plagues or disasters, any Christian communion should lose its entire ministry from within itself; or if every son to whom it may have committed the ministerial trust should prove recreant thereto and desert its standards,— by the hands of those whom it may designate as the executive of its will, it may send forth a true succession of gospel ministers. Until such an improbable, perhaps impossible, exigency arises, however, it is wise and necessary that the work of ordination be invariably performed by the highest available officer of the Christian body. Indeed, this has been done, just as far as practicable, all along. In fact, under the practical operations of the missionary and aggressive character of the gospel, Church organizations have proceeded from ministerial labors. Thus, a missionary goes into any country or community, preaches the gospel, makes converts to Christianity, and administers the sacraments. Now, they are to be organized into a compact. Who shall proceed in this business? The responsibility is plainly committed to his hands as God's minister. But he has no more right to retain and appropriate what properly belongs to others, than the employment of a common carrier, to convey goods from point to point, gives him a right of property in all the merchandise transported through his agency. On the contrary, it becomes a trust in his hands by this means, increasing the responsibility of embezzlement or malappropriation, by the character of the investiture. While, in a modified sense, the ministry forms a nucleus around which ecclesiastical organizations are collected, yet it does not exclude other and indispensable co-operative agencies in that work. The execution of legitimate ecclesiastical *authority* rests, in its ultimate analysis, upon the command of the Lord Jesus Christ, and the consent, *either formal or tacit*, of the governed. Thus the visible Church, while having, as essential to a perfect organism, the element of the consent of the parties entering into it, yet is seen to be something more than a mere voluntaryism, or voluntary association. There is in it somewhat that is anterior to the organization, and which, without the heresy of transmissionism, traces its lineage to a higher source than that of a common club or temporary association. It must be noted that the two views, transmission and derivation, are rigidly alternative grounds, and respect distinct principles of validity. One horn or the other of the dilemma must be taken. He who rejects transmission through an episcopate, and in the next breath says "the authority is in the eldership, or presbyterate," is absurdly involved in all the entanglements of difficulties which surround the doctrine of transmission. His is simply transmissionism or successionism in the eldership instead of the prelacy.

Upon Scriptural and historical ground we conclude that the ministry is commissioned to perform its functions by the body of believers—the Church—recognizing the "divine call" which originates with the Lord Jesus himself, and approbating, *i. e.*, licensing or ordaining the candidate, and thus accrediting him to the Church and the world as a gospel minister, all in the name of

Him who is the Head of the Church and the sole source of authority in his kingdom. This was the doctrine of the Reformers. When the brave John Knox was given the public office and charge of preaching, it was said: "In the body of believers, holding priesthood directly of the head, resides the sole fountain of Church power. This body corporate has a right over the gifts of its members." (Evangelical Succession, p. 47.)

Ordination being the act of the Church, it can, for what appears to it as adequate reasons, revoke the authority it confers, or such authority may be voluntarily surrendered. This is the delibility of orders. However, the solemn vow of ordination, like the divine call, upon which it is presupposedly founded, is for the whole life, and can not, therefore, be laid aside for trifling considerations or secular interests. And while it is philosophically true that "the power which gives a commission can, also, for adequate reasons, take it away," in this case the adequate reasons can be considered only in the light of the fundamental right of the Church to administer holy discipline on the basis of God's Word therefor.

Section III.

WHAT OF MINISTERIAL "ORDERS" AND OFFICERS?

The officers of the synagogue, from which the early Churches grew, may serve as a pattern;

namely, the ruler, the angel or messenger, and the minister. The former was not really an ecclesiastic at all, but was rather an officer of police or state, whose duty it was to see that the laws of the Roman government respecting assemblies were carefully observed; the second directed public services, and the latter had charge of the sacred books.

We learn from the apostolic writings that those who were fully authorized to perform ministerial functions in the early Churches are spoken of as elders, or presbyters. 1 Peter v, 1, 2: "The elders [presbyters] which are among you I exhort, who am also an elder" (presbyter) of the Church; 2 John 1: "The elder [presbyter] unto the elect lady,"—serving as examples. Among their prerogatives were to preach, administer the ordinances, and to watch over the Church; "for the perfecting of the saints, for the work of the ministry, for the edifying of the body of Christ." (Eph. iv, 12.) They have also a measure of authority in the Church: "Those elders that rule well should be counted worthy of double honor." (1 Tim. v, 17.) And the people are enjoined to "obey them that have the rule over them, and to submit themselves." (Heb. xiii, 17.) The body of elders (presbyters), it would seem, gave direction to the ordaining act, "with the laying on of the hands of the presbytery." (1 Tim. iv,

14.) That the executive *act* inheres in the eldership does not appear, however, as they were associates of the apostles in ordination: "Then it pleased the apostles and elders, with the whole Church, to send chosen men." (Acts xv, 22.) "And they wrote letters by them after this manner; The apostles and elders and brethren send greeting unto the brethren." (Acts xv, 23.)

Those who maintain that an elder (presbyter) only can confer valid orders must hold, then, that he only is an elder who has been ordained by an elder, and so on until we reach the original of the order; but this is only a renewal of personal transmission and succession in the order of elders, as real and unbroken as any claimed for apostolic succession in the order of bishops. If the line should, in any way, be once broken, it never could be restored, and the ministry, with the sacraments, must cease forever. But this would be prelacy in the eldership, as real and unmitigated as any ever claimed for episcopacy. We can not say that ministers, whether we call them presbyters or bishops, have the exclusive divine right to ordain as between themselves and Christ, themselves and the Church, and as between Christ and the Church, and, at the same time, oppose the doctrine of transmission, or apostolic succession.

There is mention also (Phil. i, 1; 1 Tim. iii, 8 and 13,) of the *deacons*, whose duties, while not very precisely defined, yet seem to have been subordinate to the apostles. The word from which it comes, and its connections, embrace generically the idea of subordination and service in sacred function. In all the history of the Church this generic idea of servitorship has been maintained. There seems to be the highly probable fact that in the Apostolic Church the deaconship was a reserve from which the elders were likely to be selected: "For they that have used the office of a deacon well purchase to themselves a good degree," etc. (1 Tim. iii, 13.) "An honorable *step.*" The word is well defined in Robinson's "Lexicon New Testament" *a step;* namely, "of a stair or door," etc., derived from *baino*, to walk or advance. Hence, unquestionably, we think Grotius gives the true meaning: "They make for themselves an honorable step; namely, to the presbyterate. For so was the custom of those ages, from the most excellent of the Christian people to select the deacons, and from the most excellent deacons the presbyters, and from the most excellent presbyters the president." In the Clementine Constitutions are prayers for the deacon, in which we read the words: "Render worthy him who has performed the deaconship to him committed inflexibly, blamelessly, unimpeachably to be exalted to a higher *step.*" The connection shows this to be the meaning. The previous verse shadows the qualifications of the eldership as the model for the deacon. The clause following these words promises a greater freedom of exercise as belonging to the next *step*. The most natural construction, certainly, should view the *step* as belonging to the sphere of the deaconship. So Wesley: "They purchase a good degree or step to some higher office." To the objection that this would be placing an objectionable motive before the deacon, Wordsworth properly replies that Paul is not addressing the deacon at all, but Timothy, the superintendent. Just so he directs Timothy (1 Tim. v, 17) "to put a double value upon the best elders." (Whedon, Com. *in loc.*)

The word *episkopos*, translated bishop, occurs five times in the New Testament. It signifies properly an overseer, one who has the inspection and oversight of anything. In 1 Peter ii, 25, we read: "For ye were as sheep going astray; but are now returned unto the Shepherd and *Bishop* of your souls." Here the element of pastoral oversight is obvious. In Acts and the Epistles we have the word as applied to certain Church officers. Acts xx, 17: "And from Miletus he [Paul] sent to Ephesus, and called the elders [presbyters] of the Church." In his address to these men (verse 28) he said: "Take heed therefore unto yourselves, and to all the flock over which the Holy Ghost hath made you overseers [*episkopous*, bishops], to feed the Church of God, which he hath purchased with his own blood." Philippians i, 1: "Paul and Timotheus, the servants of Jesus Christ, to all the saints in Christ Jesus which are at Philippi, with the bishops and deacons." 1 Tim. iii, 1, 2: "If a man desire the office of a bishop, he desireth a good work. A bishop then must be blameless." Titus i, 5–7: "For this cause left I thee in Crete, that thou shouldest set in order the things that are wanting, and ordain elders in every city, as I had appointed thee. If any be blameless, . . . for a bishop must be blameless."

Much debate has been, and is still being, indulged as to *how many orders there are in the ministry* according to constitutional requirements. Four tolerably well-defined theories have obtained, namely:

"*First. That there are constitutionally three orders in the ministry*, argued from the supposed fact that there were three orders in the Jewish priesthood. If this were true, it by no means proves that there must be three orders in the Christian ministry. Religion previous to the Savior was confessedly partial, incomplete, and cumbersome. It was a "schoolmaster to bring us unto Christ, that we might be justified by faith. But after that faith is come, we are no longer under a schoolmaster." (Gal. iii, 24, 25.) The Jewish dispensation of grace occupied the same place in religion that the spelling-book does in science and literature. An argument that will prove that there must be three orders in the ministry because there were a like number in the priesthood, will, of course, prove that there must be conformity to that system in many other respects. As, for instance, there must be the same ritual observances, the same temple service, and, in a word, that the system of Judaism must continue and Christianity be dispensed with; or, at most, that the latter is but a partial scheme superadded to the former. There can, in the nature of the case, be but two reasons given why anything in the Jewish economy of religion should be continued in the present. First, that it is a thing naturally essential in all true religion; or, second, that it has for its support the express and unmistakable command of God. Moreover, it is by no means conceded that there were three orders in the Jewish priesthood. Properly considered, there was but one order. The Levites could scarcely be called an order of priesthood. They were, more properly, the servants of the priests. "Their principal office was to wait upon the priests, and be assisting to them in the service of the tabernacle and temple; so that they were properly the ministers and servants of the priests, and obliged to obey their orders." (Horne's Introduction, Vol. II, p. 111.) The high-priest could not be said to be *an order* of priesthood, for there could be but one at a time. An order of persons can not be confined to one single person. It can not be said that one minister is an order of ministers. The term order is, at best, of very ambiguous and indefinite meaning, but this use of it would require it to serve almost any purpose. The office of high-priest is peculiar to a theocracy. He is both a civil and a religious king.

Three orders in the ministry is further attempted to be proven from the alleged fact that there were three orders of ministers in the days of the apostles. The apostles, it is said, constituted one order, the presbyters, bishops, or elders were the second, and the deacons were the third. This, however, proves too much; for the same Scripture that proves three orders will, in the same sense, prove that there were *four* or *five* or *six* orders. If the number of orders in the ministry is determined by the number of kinds or classes of ministerial labor performed by different ministers, then let us see: "And he gave some apostles, and some prophets, and some evangelists, and some pastors and teachers." (Eph. iv, 11.) Here is express mention of five different kinds of ministerial labor, in which is not mentioned either the deacon or the deaconess; so that if ministerial orders are to be reckoned in this way we have at least six or seven orders.

Second. That entire parity in the ministry is the constitutional and essential law of the Christian Church. To this it is objected that it lacks both of the only two modes of determining a constitutional provision by which it may be distinguished from a prudential regulation. First, it is not naturally necessary, in and of itself, in order to the worship of God; and, secondly, it is not expressly commanded. Again, the doctrine is impracticable. No Church can avoid—at least no Church has ever avoided—its practical infringement every day. No Church can continue to exist without the exercise of legislative, judicial, and executive functions, and nothing is more apparent in this than the necessity of conferring special authority on certain ministers—that of presidency, for instance, or power to execute laws in order to the exercise of these functions. And the moment authority is conferred upon one man which all do not possess, whether for a day, a single act, a week, a year, or a lifetime, the principle is the same—the parity is destroyed. It is not inquired in what way the principle of ministerial parity may or may not properly be disturbed, whether by the Church itself or its ministers among themselves, or for what purpose or on what occasions. Those who contend for *constitutional parity* should not complain if held to their position. Whether expediency may or may not dictate the observance of a general parity among ministers, to be disturbed only once a year, or more or less frequently, and to last only for short periods, is quite another question. That question, however, pertains to the human laws of the Church, and not to its divine constitution.

Third. That there are constitutionally two orders in the ministry, the presbyterate and the deaconry. That the episcopate is only an office in the presbyterate, and may or may not be used, as the Church may determine by its own laws. . . . If, however, God has enacted in the constitution of the Church that there *must* be two orders in the ministry, then there can not be a Church without two orders in the ministry. There must be two and only two. This is pretty high ground, and must be either maintained or abandoned. Its maintenance requires the ostracism of all Presbyterian, Episcopalian, Congregational, and, in fact, a very large proportion of all Church organisms that have ever existed. Can this be done on any ground, seeing they have, beyond all question, oftentimes given the best proofs of the presence and favor of God in the conversion of sinners among them? Again: it is certain the Church existed for a time without deacons—how long we do not know precisely—but when they were appointed it is clearly stated that it was done as an incidental measure, because of certain exigencies then present, and not as a matter essentially pertaining to the Church's existence. (See Acts vi, 1, when the deacons were selected and ordained.) The reasons for the appointment are specially set forth: first, the largeness of the Church; second, the murmuring of the Grecian or Hellenic portion of the Church.

The question is not whether the deaconry is or is not an order in the ministry; but it is, just at this point, whether to dispense with it as an order of ministry necessarily involves the forfeiture of the Church's character which she receives from God. It is whether a Church can be a Church without deaconry as an order of ministry. And we also state the objection mentioned above as a bar to the correctness of the first and the second hypotheses, viz.: that two orders in the ministry are neither naturally necessary to the worship of God and the existence of the Church, nor are they set forth in the New Testament as an essential ingredient in the Church's composition. When we lay down anything as essentially necessary to the Church's existence, we must prepare ourselves to show that in its absence the Church can not exist.

Fourth. That God established the Church in two general departments, viz., the ministry and the laity, these two divisions being essential, and their relation answering generally to that of a shepherd and his flock; but that any orders or offices or division of duties in the ministry may be varied by circumstances, times, and places, and are not essential. In other words, *one divinely constituted order of ministry, with jurisdiction allotted as the Church, the body of Christ, may direct.* "There has been a Church with a ministry since the call of Abraham at least. . . . The Christian dispensation differs from the former ones in this: that it is full, complete, and perfect as a system, and is so arranged as to adapt itself to all possible states and conditions of mankind. If we go, in our notions of constitutional adjustment, beyond the provision of a ministry, and suppose that there must be some particular *orders* or *offices* in the ministry as essentially necessary to the Church's existence, are we not likely to come in collision with some other things which are essential to the Church's catholicity? Are we right sure that it is always possible for every Church to comply with this requisition of two orders, or even to have two ministers? If we can find such a case—and they are not only possible but are really abundant—then one of two things is inevitable: either the two orders are not necessary to the Church's existence, or the system is not adapted to mankind in all possible conditions. . . . If a Church *must have* two orders in its ministry, the elders and deacons, how can this be in the case of two or three met together in the name of the Savior? This is, beyond all question, a constitutional Church. For what marks can be conceived of as defining the validity of a Church with more certainty than those which Christ has himself expressly named, viz., that the association be in *his name*, and that it have his actual presence? Here is a legal Church, and you might not be able to find in it *two orders* in its ministry." (Abbey.)

Thus, then, when we speak of different orders in the ministry, using such descriptive terms as "bishop," "elder" (or presbyter), and "deacon," we do not always mean that these gradations of rank are constitutional, necessary, inherent in the Christian Church, but that those who are admitted to the ministerial function are set apart in common for one great work, and hence belong, as a solidarity, to *one order* or class; that is, they are all generically ministers of Christ, and yet differing in allotted jurisdiction.

"In the New Testament the title of presbyter, or elder, is sometimes used as a general appellation for Church officers, including the inferior order of deacons, as it sometimes did the higher office of the apostles. Thus St. Paul gives directions to Timothy for ordaining presbyters and deacons, while in his similar directions to Titus he names presbyters only." (Dr. Jacobs.) But the apostles did not, and hence the Church is not required to, assign to all the same duties and powers when in the ministry. The constitution only requires *a* ministry, and we conclude that a Church may divide ministerial labors into as many classes as expediency may require, and these assignments may be called orders. The idea of *rank* which obtains in worldly positions is repugnant to the teaching and spirit of Christianity. However, as to what particular duties pertaining to the ministerial work should be assigned to an officer in the ministry—for example, a bishop—has been left to the discretion and godly judgment of the Christian body. And quite uniformly it has been the custom that, if we speak with reference to the *rank* of a minister, we say he belongs to the order of deacons, or presbyters; if we are considering his work, we say his is the office of a deacon or a bishop, as the case may be. "The name presbyter, or elder, expresses immediately the idea of age and of personal respectability that goes along with it, and then derivatively the idea of official dignity and authority, which are borne ordinarily by men of years and experience. The name *bishop*—that is, overseer—has regard, as the word signifies, to the official *duty* and *work* of these congregational rulers." (Schaff.)

The pastoral or *superintending* idea is absolutely essential to the idea of bishopric, the principle involved being the same whether applied to parochial or general episcopacy, and is as legitimate and more significant when applied to a superintendency over Churches in the solidarity of federation, or connectionalism, than when applied to the care of a single parish. Therefore, in the practice of the Church in general, an incumbent has been designated a presbyter, or elder, by reason of being in the ministerial class, or order, and bishop by reason of having charge, or *oversight* in the Church.

Some who have rejected the idea of an episcopate as a distinct clerical office, declare it not to be justifiable in any form by the New Testament or by Church history. However, the authority, not only of the apostles in their special and unique mission, but the authority which the Apostle Paul delegated to Timothy and Titus, may doubtless be properly considered the embryo of the episcopacy of the following age, and which has existed during all the centuries, *in various forms*, in great parts of the general Church, that being the pattern which the Churches probably followed, and which suggested the nature and measure and functions and authority which were committed to their bishops at the first. It is very apparent that the first Churches could not have been put in aggressive attitude and movement without there first having been some one specially instructed and placed in a position of supervisory control to push the work. Besides, as Churches multiplied there arose naturally a plurality of elders, or pastors, who, when they met in council or conference for the transaction of business of mutual interest, must necessarily have had a presiding officer of some kind, by whatever name he might be called. Thus in the apostolic and early post-apostolic period a moderate episcopacy was evolved, a natural development of the apostolic pattern and germ. Its perversion, however, into the prelatical idea was not known until about the close of the second century of the Christian era.

Section IV.

WHAT ARE THE PREROGATIVES OR FUNCTIONS OF THE MINISTERIAL CLASS OR ORDER?

First. As an inquiry into *its relation to the souls of the people*, two answers have obtained—the one that it is acting *for* another *with* God, or priesthood; the other that it is simply *helping* or *serving* another to come himself to God, or ministry.

Ordination, or setting apart to the sacred office, approbates or accredits the exercise of ministerial authority, but not power. It authorizes the *use* of all gifts and grace and faculties for the Church as its recognized office-bearer; but does not allege that the Church thereby confers either gifts, grace, or faculties. Spiritual power is a gift from God alone. Power of various kinds he gave in the apostolic age; but these gifts were bestowed upon men and women without any connection with, or reference to, sacred orders; and there is no intimation that ordination conferred them when possessed by ordained men in those days, even if given them at the time of their ordination. It was not by *their ordination* that they received them, but by the same means as at other times (1 Tim. iv, 14): "Neglect not the gift that is in thee, which was given thee by prophecy, with the laying on of the hands of the presbytery." This gift, no doubt, was spiritual power; but this was given to him by prophecy, *i. e.*, by express divine direction; and although it was probably given at the time of his ordination, yet it was not given by reason of the laying on of the hands of the·presbytery, but with—*i. e., together with*—this imposition of hands, the presbyters joining in the ordination, but the gift being bestowed by the hands of Paul, as in other cases—a fact which he himself mentions in his second epistle (2 Tim. i, 6), when he says: "Wherefore I put thee in remembrance, that thou stir up the gift of God, which is in thee by the putting on of my hands." The source from whence the Christian ministry is apostolically derived, and the form in which it is cast, as already presented, indicates that the clerical office is a *ministry* and not a *priesthood*. A consideration which ultimates in the same conclusion is the condition of the lay members of the Church as it appears in the New Testament, and the equality of privilege or standing-ground in Christ which Christians of all orders or degrees possessed. The fact, also, that in neither the apostolic nor any other New Testament writings, at any time whatsoever, is any Christian minister of any degree called a priest, is conclusive. In no single instance is any one of the words which describe the priesthood and its work assigned to the office of the Christian ministry or its ministrations. Words of sacerdotal meaning, while used in speaking of the priesthood of Jesus Christ, and, in a few instances *figuratively* to Christians in general, as Rom. xii, 1, "Present your bodies a living sacrifice;" also Phil. iv, 18; Heb. xiii, 15, 16; 1 Peter ii, 5, etc.; yet never so much as once are they spoken of in connection with ministerial service in the Christian Church. We learn in the Epistle to the Hebrews that from the very nature of the priestly office it is necessary for those who hold it to be specially called and appointed by God, either personally by name or according to a divinely instituted order of succession; and that since the patriarchal dispensation only two orders of priesthood have ever had this necessary divine sanction granted to them. These two orders are the *Order of Aaron* and the *Order of Melchizedek*. The priests of the former order belonged to the Jewish dispensation only, and have indisputably passed away. The only priest after the order of Melchizedek ever mentioned in the Bible is our Lord Jesus Christ, who has offered the sacrifice *once for all*. The epistle to the Hebrews shuts out the possibility of there being any other priest in the Christian Church besides Christ himself. (Dr. Jacobs, Eccl. Pol. of New Test., p. 106.) Those who assume to be priests after the order of Melchizedek are guilty of an impious claim. Without foundation equally is the artifice that the clergy as a representative order, and delegates from the whole Christian community, are priestly in their office; for there is no ground for a moment to suppose that priestly functions and privileges of the Christian people ever were or can be thus transferred or delegated. To call a gospel minister a priest is a gross perversion and abuse of the term. He is simply ordained of God for the evangelization of the world, the maintenance of sound doctrine, and the edification of the people in due proportion of faith, the conducting of religious worship with becoming solemnity and reverence, the administration of the ordinances, and the promotion of the glory of God.

Second. As an inquiry into *its relation to the administering of the affairs of the Church* two answers also have obtained, some averring that the power is inherent in the ministerial office, others that a large proportion of it belongs to the laity. The broad claims of the clergy in past time, and the large concessions made to them, have naturally had the effect to run the first opinion into a dangerous extreme. On the other hand, the strong preference for republicanism, or for democracy even, especially in this country, together with the popular assumption that the Church is purely a voluntary association, deriving all its authority from the free consent of those entering into it, and having, therefore, full power to that effect, and ought to be modeled after the popular civil democracies of the time, has carried many to the opposite extreme.

Predicating, first, that the body of believers has a right to make rules and regulations for its own government, in harmony with the principles therefor in the Word of God, we may safely say that it will probably be found in this case, as in most others, that truth and safety lie between the extremes. It is evident that something in the nature of ecclesiastical authority is recognized as antecedent to Church organization, which, therefore, in a sense, is a nucleus around which such organizations must form, and that this authority is originally vested in the ministry of the gospel. In granting this, however, nothing is yielded to overgrown ministerial claims. To find out determinately the nature and extent of the foundation and general elements of ministerial authority, we must look chiefly to the commission of Christ, by which the gospel ministry was itself instituted. The Lord Jesus, after stating his right to confer such authority, based on the possession of "all power in heaven and on earth," proceeds to ordain the following things in relation to the ministry:

1. That it shall be universal in its range of action: "Go ye into all nations." 2. That it shall be perpetual: "I am with you to the *end of the world.*" 3. That its first great business is to preach and teach, and so make disciples: "Preach the gospel to every creature, . . . teaching them to observe all things whatsoever I have commanded you." 4. That another and sequent duty of the ministry is to administer to those they shall have discipled the initiatory sacrament of baptism, thereby receiving them into the Christian Church: "Baptizing them in the name of

the Father, the Son, and the Holy Ghost." 5. The ministry is required to enforce faith in Christ as the great condition of salvation: "He that believeth and is baptized shall be saved, and he that believeth not shall be damned." Here the sacred trust is committed to the ministry of making disciples to Christ by preaching the gospel, and of receiving their converts into the Christian Church.

How were the apostles to receive members into the Church when as yet the Christian Church was not formally instituted? Plainly a commission and command to impart all gospel teaching, and to apply to the taught the initiatory sacrament, carried with it, by necessary and unavoidable implication, all the incidental powers required for the perfecting of the organization clearly contemplated by the commission. And this has always been the case under the operations of missionary effort, a necessary result of the aggressive character of the gospel.

The conclusion, therefore, is fair, that in whatever belongs distinctively to the powers and duties of the ministry the laity have no right to a share or participation; nor have the ministry any right to yield to the claim if it were made; the trust is not negotiable. But with regard to all those acts that are contributory to the great ends of gospel ministry all should alike be participants. The lay Christian has, in virtue of his relation to Christ and his invisible Church, a graciously inherent valid claim to participate in all those rights in the visible Church which Christ has not vested elsewhere. And a Church in its formative stage might, to be sure, resolve that there shall be no pope, no cardinal, no prelatical bishop, and the like, because no restriction exists at that point; but it could not resolve that there shall be no ministry, no exercise of discipline, no sacraments, because such a statute would be void for unconstitutionality.

In the New Testament ideal of the Church, while all members have not the same office (Rom. xii, 4, 5), it is as consistent with the absolute freedom, and the enjoyment of the real rights of every member of the Church, as are the offices of senator and representative, named in the American Constitution, with the liberties of every citizen of the Republic. "The *hoodlum* or communistic demand that all organism in Church or State shall be ground to its component dust, to its ultimate atoms, is without brains as it is without God. The *hoodlum* in Church or State is himself an organism, and logically annihilates himself in his *insane* 'All-on-a-level' cry—'No officers!' 'No authority!'" (Perrine.)

"The apostolic or New-Testament Church was not simply a mechanical mass, an aggregation of individual Christians. It was an organism, a personality—the living 'body of Christ.' In the distribution of specific functions to particular members of this organism, the triumph of the division-of-labor principle was never more complete. . . . Nothing here is generic; every thing is specific. No Jacobinic leveling, no atheistic communism; but a sublime personality, a mighty moral organism, the body of Christ, in which wondrous synthesis of 'members in particular' every specific function is to be performed by its own particular organ." (Perrine.)

Let it not be for one moment supposed that the analyses which run through this chapter are in the interest of some definite and specific form of Church government, for they are not. They are but the setting forth of some general principles which evidently obtained in the apostolic Church. Absolute uniformity in all the details of Church visibility is neither declared nor required. "In the days of the apostles the several forms of Church government were not specifically defined, arranged, and understood as they are now. This could not have been the case, for the experience of the Church was not sufficient for such a precise classification of the elements of government, as all men readily recognize. They acted in regard to government, from time to time, and in places here and in places there, as circumstances seemed to justify or render expedient. . . . Hence, in their ecclesiastical proceeding we find somewhat of all the several elements of government usually applied to Churches, as men have since those days classified and defined these several elementary principles. We see supervisory control over ministers and Churches; that is episcopacy. We see as to an entire equality among ministers; that is Presbyterianism. We see congregations governing themselves independently; that is Congregationalism. We see ministers and laymen mingling together, consulting, determining, and electing to office; that is republicanism. . . . Hence we conclude that the acts and doings of the apostles and their fellow-Christians, even where we are able to trace them with certainty, do not form specific and determinate directions for Christians in all after time, except it be in the following cases: When such actions, in the nature of the thing, pertain to religious truth and conduct, in all possible human circumstances. When they amount to specific command coming from the Savior through the apostles. When such acts clearly amount to an institution of the gospel." (Abbey.)

George P. Fisher, D. D., LL. D., professor of ecclesiastical history in Yale University, in his recent Dudleian lecture on the "Validity of Non-episcopal Ordination," said: "That no specific form of Church government can boast of being an apostolic ordinance for all time, is a verdict which historical scholars are rapidly approaching unanimity in rendering. The divine right of a particular form of Church organization will follow the divine right of kings, and repose in the same tomb." (Page 30.)

So great an historian as Mosheim declares (Vol. I, chap. ii, sec. 5) that "the details of a specific and definite order of Church polity were not prescribed by either Christ or the apostles."

Investiture with authority to do a particular work carries with it the power to do all rightful things for its accomplishment. To those upon whom it devolved to promulge the gospel it was left to arrange, by a divinely guided judgment, these or those regulations to that end, adjusting ecclesiastical arrangements and constructing canons in harmony with the doctrines, spirit, designs, and constitutional principles of the gospel, consulting a true Christian expediency; and an expediency is only truly Christian when inherently and intrinsically right in harmony with the Word and for the glory of God.

The conclusion to which the facts set forth in this chapter bring us is, in brief, the definition with which it begins. Therefore any body of believers, providentially called together to that end, associating on the basis of the Christian faith and for the realization of its ends, is as truly a Church—an apostolic organism—as any that ever graced the globe; and the ministry which it may set apart as truly apostolic as any that ever administered in the name of the Lord. Such are some of the principles of a truly COMPREHENSIVE CHURCH.

Part Two.

HARMONY OF METHODIST EPISCOPAL GENESIS
AND ORDER WITH THE PRECEDENTS
AND PRINCIPLES OF THE
NEW TESTAMENT.

PRELIMINARY.

GENERAL principles have particular applications. The doctrines of Derivation is a general principle. Its particular application to the great reformed, Protestant, and evangelical bodies of believers is apparent in the incipient history of each.

The purpose of Part II is to show the conformity of the Methodist Episcopal organism to that which is apostolic, and that it is, therefore, an apostolic organism.

Apostolic Organism.

CHAPTER I.

DEVELOPMENT AND FORMATION OF THE METHODIST EPISCOPAL CHURCH.

"THE roots of the present," it has been said, "lie deep in the past, and nothing in the past is dead to the man who would learn how the present comes to be what it is." "When we understand," it has been further said, "how any thing *has become* what *it is*, we understand its *history*. Indeed, its history is the process of *becoming* what *it is*, and the record of this process constitutes its recorded history." He who will learn how Methodism has become what it is, will perceive as others can not its providential incipiency, and the wonderful mission which the Head of the Church has set before it.

Louis XIV, king of France, in his excessive devotion to papal dominance, had revoked the Edict of Nantes, granted by Henry IV for the toleration of the Protestants, and suppressed their worship, demolished their churches, and banished their ministers. Among the five hundred thousand of the most industrious and useful subjects of France, lost to her by this weak, impolitic measure of the king, were the German dwellers in the Palatinate on the Rhine, who, driven before the papal troops, found refuge within the lines of the duke of Marlborough, and were provided for by Anne, queen of Great Britain, some in England, some in Ireland, and some in America. Among the expatriated ones in Ireland, in 1758, John Wesley found in the county of Limerick a community, still speaking their Teutonic tongue, who had for almost a half century been pastorless, and had become thoroughly demoralized, formerly noted for drunkenness, profanity, and "utter neglect of religion," but whose hamlets had been penetrated by the Methodist itinerants who had traveled that way, and who, under God, were raising up there a reformed and devout people. They had erected a large chapel in the center of their population, and Mr. Wesley says there was "no cursing or swearing, no Sabbath-breaking, no drunkenness, no ale-house. They had become a serious, thinking people, and their diligence had turned all their land into a garden. How will these poor foreigners," he adds, "rise up in the day of judgment against those that are round about them!" In August, 1760, a vessel arrived at New York having on board a group of these "Palatines," as these German-Irishmen were usually called, among them Philip Embury, thoughtful and modest, who had heard John Wesley preach in Ireland in 1752, and was converted thereby on Christmas day of that year, and was soon after licensed a local preacher; and also Barbara Heck, "a mother in Israel" truly. She it was who, roused by righteous indignation against sin, in 1766, had urged the modest and shrinking Embury to preach to their people, but a few of whom were Wesleyans, which he did, in his own house, and so is the first American Methodist preacher and class-leader. Here was the germ from which, in the good providence of God, sprung the Methodist movement in America.

It is interesting to note that the distinguishing term *Methodist* was not one newly coined, but was an old one revived. There had existed in the century immediately preceding the Christian era a school of physicians, founded probably by Themison, who is referred to by Juvenal. This school of medical practice discarded the empirical method and mere observations of phenomenan, and held to the pure deductions of reason and logic from certain premises. They took the name *Methodist*—Greek, *Methodikos*, "that acts by regular rules, treats a subject according to certain rules" (Donnegan)—thereby conveying the idea of their strict adherence to logical processes. Their success in medical practice is not reported. Had it, however, been very unsuccessful, it is not probable it would have been sufficiently extensive to have become almost proverbial, as must appear from the classic authors. The term had been applied also, it appears, about a hundred years before the formation of the Holy Club at Oxford University, by the Wesleys and others, to Non-conformists "for their views respecting the method of man's justification before God." Accordingly, when the young gentlemen of the club were studying the Greek New Testament for spiritual purposes, by reason of the exactness and regularity of their lives, as well as studies, a student of Christ's Church College called out: "Here is a new set of Methodists sprung up!" The term being new to the popular ear, and strikingly quaint, the Methodists were known all over the university. Thus the name now so familiar in all the world began. Those to whom it was given had no purpose of introducing to the world any new ecclesiastical institutes, as they were zealous and devoted members of the Church of England, nor to formulate any new doctrines, but to live out consistently to their logical sequences the doctrines of the New Testament as they had been accepted by evangelical Christians from the beginning. Subsequently, when John Wesley published his dictionary for

"The People called Methodists," he defined the name as meaning "one who lives according to the method laid down in the Holy Scriptures."

Section I.

ORGANIC ACT AND PRINCIPLES.

Lovely Lane Chapel, Baltimore, Maryland, Christmas week, A. D. 1784, was the scene of one of the most important and remarkable religious convocations ever assembled. It was the culminating point of seventeen preceding synodical gatherings, or conferences, which had been held, from time to time, during the ten preceding years. The enactments of these bodies were not final until they had become the expression of the majority of the ministry in the connection, together with that of the General Assistant, or the superintending officer, acting under the appointment and direction of Rev. John Wesley, A. M., under God, the founder-apostle of the Methodist societies. The infant Churches of American Methodism were at that time called simply societies, because of the absence of an ordained ministry as yet to administer the holy sacraments therein. In May, 1779, a regular conference had been held in Fluvanna County, Virginia, in which the question, "Shall we administer the ordinances?" which had been long agitated, was answered affirmatively, to the great satisfaction of what had come to be known as the "sacramental party"—one of the principal reasons for determining the controversy being, "the Episcopal Establishment is now dissolved in this country, and therefore, in almost all our circuits, the members are without the ordinances." Therefore the Fluvanna Conference appointed "a committee," and constituted it "a presbytery," first, to administer the ordinances themselves; second, to authorize any other preacher or preachers, approved by them by the form of laying on of hands.

Stevens says (History of the Methodist Episcopal Church, Vol. II, pp. 64, 65): "Lee impartially records the facts of the controversy, though he evidently sympathizes with the Fluvanna brethren. In the course of this year, he says, they 'concluded that if God had called them to preach the gospel, he had called them also to administer the ordinances of baptism and the Lord's Supper. They chose a committee for the purpose of ordaining ministers. The preachers ordained went forth preaching the gospel in their circuits as formerly, and administered the sacraments wherever they went, provided the people were willing to partake with them. Most of our preachers in the South fell in with this new plan; and as the leaders of the party were very zealous, and the greater part of them very pious men, the private members were influenced by them, and pretty generally fell in with their measures; however, some of the old Methodists would not commune with them, but steadily adhered to their old customs. The preachers north of Virginia were opposed to this step, so hastily taken by their brethren in the South, and made a stand against it, believing that, unless a stop could be put to this new mode of proceeding, a separation would take place among the preachers and the people. There was great cause to fear a division, and both parties trembled for the ark of God, and shuddered at the thought of dividing the Church of Christ. The preachers in the South were very successful in their ministerial labors, and many souls were brought to God in the latter part of the year. These things all united to confirm them in the belief that the step they had taken was honored of God. And at that time there was very little room to hope that they would ever recede from their new plan, in which they were so well established. But, after all, they consented, for the sake of peace and the union of the body of Methodists, to drop the ordinances for a season, till Mr. Wesley could be consulted.'"

This statement of facts shows how thoroughly the Methodist sentiment was with the doctrine of derivation. It should be noted that there is a direct connection with these events and those which soon after occurred in England, and that the American Methodists were as much a party to those events as could be possible with the intervening space of the ocean between the parties to the transaction.

In Bristol, England, September 1, 1784, Rev. John Wesley, Thomas Coke, and James Creighton, presbyters of the Church of England, formed a presbytery and ordained Richard Whatcoat and Thomas Vasey deacons; and on September 2d, by the same hands, etc., Richard Whatcoat and Thomas Vasey were ordained elders, and Thomas Coke, D. C. L., was ordained superintendent for the Church of God under their care in North America.

In due process of providential guidance, we find assembled in aforesaid Lovely Lane Chapel, in Baltimore, on Christmas eve, 1784, sixty out of the eighty-one itinerant preachers of the Methodist societies, a legal majority of the recognized legislators. They have come from both the North and the South. In obscurity, if not ignominy, amid poverty, persecutions, and public strifes of politics and arms that had swept over them like tempests, these men had wrought, and had laid, stone by stone, the foundations for an ecclesiastical edifice. It is well that they should assemble to consider what the structure should be, and, under God, to erect the same.

On taking the chair, Doctor Coke presented a letter from Wesley, dated Bristol, September 10, 1784, and addressed: "To Dr. Coke, Mr. Asbury, and our Brethren in North America." It said: "By a very uncommon train of providences, many of the provinces of North America are totally disjoined from the British Empire and erected into independent States. The English government has no authority over them, either civil or ecclesiastical, any more than over the States of Holland. A civil authority is exercised over them partly by the Congress, partly by the State Assemblies. But no one either exercises or claims any ecclesiastical authority at all. In this peculiar situation some thousands of the inhabitants of these States desire my advice, and, in compliance with their desire, I have drawn up a little sketch. Lord King's 'Account of the Primitive Church' convinced me, many years ago, that bishops and presbyters are the same order, and, consequently, have the same right to ordain. For many years I have been importuned, from time to time, to exercise this right by ordaining part of our traveling preachers; but I have still refused, not only for peace' sake, but because I was determined, as little as possible, to violate the established order of the National Church, to which I belonged. But the case is widely different between England and North America.

Here there are bishops who have a legal jurisdiction. In America there are none, and but few parish ministers; so that for some hundred miles together there is none either to baptize or to administer the Lord's Supper. Here, therefore, my scruples are at an end, and I conceive myself at full liberty, as I violate no order and invade no man's right, by appointing and sending laborers into the harvest. I have, accordingly, appointed Dr. Coke and Mr. Francis Asbury to be joint *superintendents* over our brethren in North America; as also Richard Whatcoat and Thomas Vasey to act as *elders* among them by baptizing and administering the Lord's Supper. If any one will point out a more rational and Scriptural way of feeding and guiding those poor sheep in the wilderness I will gladly embrace it. At present I can not see any better method than that I have taken. It has, indeed, been proposed to desire the English bishops to ordain part of our preachers for America. But to this I object, 1. I desired the bishop of London to ordain one only, but could not prevail. 2. If they consented, we know the slowness of their proceedings, but the matter admits of no delay. 3. If they would ordain them now, they would likewise expect to govern them. And how grievously would this entangle us! 4. As our American brethren are now totally disentangled, both from the State and from the English hierarchy, we dare not entangle them again either with the one or the other. They are now at full liberty simply to follow the Scriptures and the primitive Church. And we judge it best that they should stand fast in that liberty wherewith God has so strangely made them free."

Here was a "providential call." Never was necessity more dire. Never did Continental or English reformers have such occasion to declare that "necessity has no law."

The organizing convocation had before it, in the exercise of its Scriptural right of deciding by what form the Methodist people would govern themselves, the various forms described in the Preliminary to Part I.

In accordance with the letter of Mr. Wesley, "it was agreed," says Francis Asbury, "to form ourselves into an Episcopal Church, and to have superintendents, elders, and deacons," the Minutes of proceedings reading thus: "Question 3. As the ecclesiastical as well as civil affairs of these United States have passed through a very considerable change by the Revolution, what plan of Church government shall we hereafter pursue? Answer. We will form ourselves into an Episcopal Church, under the direction of superintendents, elders, deacons, and helpers, according to the forms of ordination annexed to our Liturgy and the form of Discipline set forth in these Minutes." (History of the Discipline, Emory, p. 27.)

In the Discipline of 1789, section 3, setting forth the nature and constitution of the new organization, after a preamble setting forth the historic facts, it is said: "For these reasons we have thought it our duty to form ourselves into an independent Church. And as the most excellent mode of Church government, according to our maturest judgment, is that of a *moderate episcopacy*, and as we are persuaded that the uninterrupted succession of bishops from the apostles can be proved neither from Scripture nor antiquity, we therefore have constituted ourselves into an Episcopal Church, under the direction of bishops, elders, deacons, and preachers, according to the forms of ordination annexed to our Prayer-book and the regulations laid down in this form of Discipline." (Ibid., p. 93.)

Thus begging no privilege, making no excuses, framing no apologies, fawning at the feet of no worldly congress or parliament, but recognizing the apostolic principles of the Church as *a covenanted compact of believers as such*, and standing upon their inherent, God-given, New Testament, apostolic rights, under the presidency of the Lord Jesus Christ, the sole Head and Sovereign of the Church, the only source of any authority claimed in behalf of all who were eligible to the associative compact; namely, the fifteen thousand members and eighty-one preachers of the American Methodist societies by their associative act, their covenanted compact, as expressed by their own free vote in the organizing convention, the famous Christmas Conference, performed THE act by which those in the compact stood forth as an organic portion of the Church catholic and visible.

In performing this organic act, a distinguishing appellation must be chosen. It should be one which will indicate distinctive character. The use of affixes and prefixes takes Scriptural precedent. It is true that the only name given by the mouth of the Lord to his organic people is simply Church, the first mention in the New Testament being Matt. xvi, 18. However, the apostles addressed their epistles in a manner which characterized or indicated certain portions of it, as "The Church in thy house," "The Church of God," "Unto the Church of the Thessalonians." "The seven Churches of Asia" were Ephesus, Smyrna, Pergamos, Thyatira, Sardis, Philadelphia, Laodicea. Those who claim some divinely given name other than, and in addition to, the term church, and themselves non-sectarian because they have adopted it, have failed to make the claim good, it not being demonstrable that "the disciples were first called Christians at Antioch" other than in derision. Certain it is, the name could not have been understood by the disciples to be divine, else would they have used it when in their apostolic office they wrote the Churches. The name is used but three times in the New Testament, and never as a prefix or descriptive appellation to the word church.* Therefore the organizing body followed an apostolic pattern, in the use of an appellative term, distinctly descriptive. As already noted, this people were already known as *Methodists*, because they walked by rule. Having now adopted moderate episcopacy as the mode by which they should administer government over themselves, they are *episcopal;* what more fitting, and Scriptural, too, than that the new organism shall be designated as the *Methodist Episcopal* Church?

Thus it stood forth the first Protestant Episcopal Church organized upon the American continent. Dr. Coke arrived in New York eleven days prior to the ordination of Dr. Seabury by the Jacobites, or non-jurors, and entered upon the American episcopate Christmas week, 1784,

---

*The edifice in which a Church, or assembly, worships is, in common usage, called a church, on the rhetorical law which allows the thing which contains to be known by the name of the thing contained. Such is the possible use of 1 Cor. xi, 18: "For first of all, when ye come together in the church," etc. The word indicating temple is also translated by the word church, Acts xix, 37.

while the latter did not come into authority in his diocese in Connecticut until August, 1785, and in the Protestant Episcopal Church until 1789, when he acted with the other bishops in the consecration of Rev. T. Claggett, D. D., as bishop of Maryland, the first bishop consecrated by that body in America. However, this assertion of historic seniority and any claims of birthright by reason of this priority, are not made with any assumptions of "High-Church divinity or high-starch dignity," nor with any prettiness of prattle or daintiness of dialect about " churchly," " unchurchly," " churchliness," etc., but with a hearty cordiality of Christian fraternity and fellowship in the name of our common Lord.

That the organization of the Methodist Episcopal Church was on the New Testament principle, described herein as derivationism, is apparent to all. That such has continued to be the principle upon which action has proceeded is seen in the utterances of representative Methodists—*e. g.*, "A Church is simply an associate body of the believers (the two or three met in the name of Christ, and the Master among them), competent to organize itself without other helps." (Daniel Curry, D. D., in *National Repository*.) "A Church is simply a spontaneous aggregation of Christian believers, ordering themselves into such organic form as may best attain the ends of their own salvation and the universal spread of Christian holiness." (D. D. Whedon, LL. D., in *Methodist Quarterly Review*.)

From the day when that "elect lady," Barbara Heck, appealed to Philip Embury to preach to their Teuton-Celtic friends, and the first associative compact called "a class," to this, has *fellowship on the basis of the Christian faith*, or associating by covenant compacts, been regarded as the germ of organic or visible Church life, and the individual initiative thereto, the Church covenant accepted by all running thus: "Here, in the presence of God and of this congregation, I renew the solemn promise contained in the baptismal covenant, ratifying and confirming the same, and acknowledging myself bound faithfully to observe and keep the same. I here profess saving faith in the Lord Jesus Christ. I believe in the doctrines of Holy Scripture as set forth in the Articles of Religion of the Methodist Episcopal Church. I will cheerfully be governed by the rules of the Methodist Episcopal Church, hold sacred the ordinances of God, and endeavor, as much as in me lies, to promote the welfare of my brethren and the advancement of the Redeemer's kingdom. I will contribute of my earthly substance, according to my ability, to the support of the gospel and the various benevolent enterprises of the Church."

While recognizing that *the application of holy discipline, on the basis of the rules therefor in God's Holy Word,* is an essential prerogative of a Church, yet those who enter this communion and fellowship do not do so because of any real or supposed authority over them beyond that to which they voluntarily assent for the mutual welfare, and from which compact, if they ultimately dissent, they may withdraw, but because with its doctrines they mainly *agree;* and with its governmental arrangements and prudential and instituted means of grace they cordially *coincide.* They greatly love and warmly defend the organism because it helpfully promotes piety, and piety, in its turn, conserves orthodoxy and Church loyalty. Continuance in this fellowship is conditional upon correctness of life; and hence, that the purity and credit of the Church may be guarded, a Scripturally balanced judicial system has been maintained, of which Matt. xviii, 15–17, is the basis, its prerogative being to maintain the orderliness of the body in membership and ministry. No claim is made of right to inflict pains and penalties, as in civil governments; for the only punitive discipline authorized in the New Testament is comprised in "admonition," "reproof," "sharp rebukes," and, finally, "excision from the society," as St. Paul expresses it (1 Cor. v, 13), to "put away"—all this to preserve a spiritual Church on the faith of the gospel, experimentally and practically held. And the attainment of this moral end is by moral means. And as our Lord treated even "heathens and publicans" with compassion and kindness, and sought their salvation, so much the more the separated and disowned brother is still the object of charity and sympathy, and every means taken to effect his restoration in the spirit of Him who said: "Brethren, if a man be overtaken in a fault, ye which are spiritual restore such a one in the spirit of meekness." (Gal. vi, 1.) This is in wide contrast with ecclesiastical anathemas, thumb-screws, wheels, and firebrands.

That *the sacraments should be administered according to Christ's ordinance, in those things that are requisite to the same*, was incorporated into the very constitution of the Methodist Episcopal Church as of divine appointment, the sixteenth, seventeenth, eighteenth, and nineteenth of her Articles of Religion, and her uniform practice from the beginning, fully attest. Baptism, the sacrament of the Holy Spirit, being instituted and made obligatory (Matt. xxviii, 19), and indorsed and perpetuated by apostolic practice (Acts ii, 1–41; viii, 26–39; ix, 18; and xxii, 16; x, 44–48; and xi, 15, 16; xvi, 13–15; xvi, 30–34); and the Lord's Supper, the sacrament of the Son being instituted and made obligatory (Matt. xxvi, 26–28;

Luke xxii, 19), and indorsed and perpetuated by apostolic sanction and commendation (1 Cor. xi, 24, 25), were received as the ONLY sacraments instituted by Christ, and are practiced according to his command. In these "outward signs of an inward grace," we have an exhibition and adumbration of the whole system of grace, a summary of the doctrines and precepts of the everlasting gospel, so that through the senses the heart is affected and instructed, and at suitably recurring periods is reminded of personal relations and obligations to God.

This Church receives the canonical Scriptures as the only and sufficient rule of faith and practice, open, unfettered, in the hands of the people, the words of the inspired apostles of the first century being more trustworthy and of plainer import than the comments thereon of the uninspired self-styled successors of those apostles in the nineteenth century. The final appeal, in all matters of doctrine, experience, and practice, is to the divine plenary authority of the Holy Scriptures; the twenty-five Articles of Religion, really an expansion of the twelve items of the Apostles' Creed—the creed of Christendom—and other "standards of doctrine" setting forth a distinctive theological platform, in harmony with the Methodist watchcry, "Spread Scriptural holiness over these lands!"

"I have lived," says the learned Dr. Adam

Clarke, under date of July 26, 1832, "more than threescore years and ten; I have traveled a great deal, both by sea and land; I have conversed with and seen many people, in and from different countries; I have studied the principal religious systems in the world; I have read much, thought much, and reasoned much; and the result is, I am persuaded of the simple, unadulterated truth of no book but the Bible, and of the true excellence of no system of religion but that contained in the Holy Scriptures; and especially *Christianity*, which is referred to in the Old Testament and fully revealed in the New. And while I think well of, and wish well to, all religious sects and parties, and especially to all who love our Lord Jesus Christ in sincerity, yet, from a long and thorough knowledge of the subject, I am led, most conscientiously, to conclude that Christianity itself, as existing among those called Wesleyan Methodists, is the purest, the safest, that which is most to God's glory and the benefit of man; and *that*, both as to the creed there professed, form of discipline there established, and the consequent moral practice there vindicated. And I believe that among them is to be found the best form and body of divinity that has ever existed in the Church of Christ, from the promulgation of Christianity to the present day. To him who would say, 'Dr. Clarke, are you not a bigot?' without hesitation I would answer, 'No, I am not; for, by the grace of God, I am a Methodist!' Amen."

Section II.

RELATION OF JOHN WESLEY TO THE ORGANIC ACT.

This has received a partial consideration in the preceding section. It should receive further attention, however, inasmuch as both those who persist in supposing an undescribed, and indeed indescribable, halo to crown an episcopate which assumes to have descended according to transmissionism and those who reject all episcopal systems whatever, ask how could Mr. Wesley give an episcopate since he was not himself a bishop. Then to the facts.

The Discipline of the Methodist Episcopal Church, in 1789, in section 4, "On constituting of bishops, and their duty," says:

"Question 1. What is the proper origin of the episcopal authority in our Church? Answer. In the year 1784 the Rev. John Wesley, who, under God, has been the father of the great revival of religion now extending over the earth by the means of the Methodists, determined, at the intercession of multitudes of his spiritual children on this continent, to ordain ministers for America, and for this purpose sent over three regularly ordained clergy; but, preferring the Episcopal mode of Church government to any other, solemnly set apart, by the imposition of his hands and prayer, one of them; namely, Thomas Coke, doctor of civil law, late of Jesus' College, in the University of Oxford, for the episcopal office; and having delivered to him letters of episcopal orders, commissioned and directed him to set apart Francis Asbury, then general assistant of the Methodist Society in America, for the same episcopal office, he, the said Francis Asbury, being first ordained deacon and elder; in consequence of which the said Francis Asbury was solemnly set apart for the said episcopal office by prayer and the imposition of the hands of the said Thomas Coke, other regularly ordained ministers assisting in the sacred ceremony. At which time the General Conference, held at Baltimore, did unanimously receive the said Thomas Coke and Francis Asbury as their bishops, being fully satisfied of the validity of their episcopal ordination." (History of the Discipline, pp. 93, 94.)

It is to be noted that the basis of the authority in this action was "the intercession of multitudes of the spiritual children" of Rev. John Wesley "on this continent to ordain ministers for America," and the fact that "the General Conference, held at Baltimore, did unanimously *receive* the said Thomas Coke and Francis Asbury as their bishops, being fully satisfied of the validity of their episcopal ordination." It was the Church, the covenanted compact of believers, that ordained; and upon such grounds is the episcopacy still maintained and regulated, "BY THE AUTHORITY OF THE CHURCH." (*Cf.* Ritual for Consecration of Bishops.)

In their Notes to the Discipline, by Bishops Coke and Asbury, published in the Discipline of 1796, and receiving the implied sanction of the General Conference of 1800, in section 1, "Of the Origin of the Methodist Episcopal Church," they say: "It can not be needful in this country to vindicate the right of every Christian society to possess within itself all the privileges necessary or expedient for the comfort, instruction, or good government of the members thereof. The two sacraments of Baptism and the Lord's Supper have been allowed to the formation of a Christian Church, by every party and denomination in every age and country of Christendom, with the exception only of a single modern society; and ordination by the imposition of hands has been allowed to be highly expedient, and has been practiced as universally as the former. And these two points, as above described, might, if need were, be confirmed by the Scriptures, and by the unanimous testimony of all the primitive fathers of the Church for the three first centuries, and, indeed, by all the able divines who have written on the subject in the different languages of the world down to the present times."

The only point which can be disputed by any sensible person, is the *episcopal* form which we have adopted; and this can be contested by *candid* men only from their want of acquaintance with the history of the Church. The most bigoted devotees to religious establishments—the clergy of the Church of Rome excepted—are now ashamed to support the doctrine of *the apostolic, uninterrupted succession of bishops.* Dr. Hoadley, bishop of Winchester, who was, we believe, the greatest advocate for episcopacy whom the Protestant Churches ever produced, has been so completely overcome by Dr. Calamy, in respect to the uninterrupted succession, that the point has been entirely given up. Nor do we recollect that any writer of the Protestant Churches has since attempted to defend what all the learned world at present know to be utterly indefensible. And yet nothing but *an apostolic, uninterrupted succession* can possibly confine the right of episcopacy to any particular Church. The idea that the supreme magistrate or legislature of a country ought to be the head of the Church in that nation, is a position which, we think, no one *here* will presume to assert. It follows, therefore, indubitably that every Church has a right to choose, if it please, the episcopal plan.

The late Rev. John Wesley recommended the *episcopal* form to his societies in America, and the General Conference, which is the chief synod of our Church, unanimously accepted of it. Mr. Wesley did more. He first consecrated one for the office of a bishop that our episcopacy might descend from himself. The General Conference unanimously accepted of the person so consecrated, as well as of Francis Asbury, who had for many years before exercised every branch of the episcopal office, excepting that of ordination. Now, the idea of an apostolic succession being exploded, it follows that the Methodist Church has everything which is Scriptural and essential to justify its episcopacy. Is the unanimous approbation of the chief synod of a Church necessary? This it has had. Is the ready compliance of the members of the Church with its decision in this respect necessary? This it has had and continues to have. Is it highly expedient that the fountain of episcopacy should be respectable? This has been the case. The most respectable divine since the primitive ages, if not since the time of the apostles, was Mr. Wesley. His knowledge of the sciences was very extensive. He was a general scholar; and for any to call his learning in question would be to call their own. On his death the literati of England bore testimony to his great character. And where has been the individual so useful in the spread of religion? But in this we can appeal only to the lovers of *vital* godliness. By his long and incessant labors he raised a multitude of societies, who looked up to him for direction; and certainly his direction in things lawful, with the full approbation of the people, was sufficient to give authenticity to what was accordingly done. He was peculiarly attached to the laws and customs of the Church in the primitive times of Christianity. He knew that the primitive Churches universally followed the episcopal plan; and, indeed, Bishop Hoadley has demonstrated that the episcopal plan was universal till the time of the Reformation. Mr. Wesley, therefore, preferred the *episcopal* form of Church government; and God has (glory be to his name!) wonderfully blessed it among us.

But in all that we have observed on this subject, we by no means intend to speak disrespectfully of the Presbyterian Church, nor of any other. We only desire to defend our own from the unjust calumnies of its opponents.

Hooker, a high authority on ecclesiastical order in the Church of England, said: "There may be sometimes very just and sufficient reasons to allow ordination without a bishop. *The whole Church visible being the true original subject of all power*, it hath not ordinarily allowed any other than bishops alone to ordain. Howbeit, as the ordinary cause is ordinary in all things to be observed, so it may be, in some cases, not unnecessary that we decline from the ordinary ways. Men may be extraordinarily, yet allowably, in two ways admitted into spiritual functions in the Church. One is when God himself doth of himself raise up a way; another, when the exigency of necessity doth constrain to leave the usual ways of the Church, which otherwise we would willingly keep." (Ecclesiastical Polity, viii, 14.)

Again: "Let them [the bishops] continually bear in mind that it is rather the force of custom whereby the Church, having so long found it good to continue the regiment of her virtuous bishops, doth still uphold, maintain, and honor them in that respect than that any true and heavenly law can be showed by the evidence whereof it may be a truth appear that the Lord himself hath appointed presbyters forever to be under regiment of bishops." (Ibid., vii, 5.)

In complete accordance with the doctrine of this great standard author, "the judicious Hooker," did Wesley establish intentionally and truly the episcopacy of American Methodism; for,

First. He was a presbyter of the Church of England, a grade of ministry in which the right to ordain inheres, although ordination by an elder is not by the "Church visible" "ordinarily allowed." The only question, then, is whether that "exigency of necessity" existed calling for an extraordinary ordination by a presbyter in this case of Wesley.

Second. This extraordinary call did exist in more ways than one.

1. There existed a great people, the substance and material of an inchoate Church, founded by Mr. Wesley himself, demanding from his hand a form of government. For four years Wesley declined to obey that demand, and furnish the organizing act, by which delay the people were left without polity and without the sacraments of Christ.

2. The bishops of the Church of England entirely neglected Wesley's request for an ordination by their hands; and even if they were willing, there was great danger that their hand would, in fact, repress the great work. The very safety and continued existence of this revival, and the continuance of this people, required that he who, under Providence, founded their order should shape their form and guide their movements in accordance with their past history.

3. As there was thus an external call and exigent "necessity," so there doubtless was a divine call—not miraculous, but by movement of the blessed Spirit to this work. And so Wesley him-

self, in his episcopal diploma to Coke, declared: "I, John Wesley, think myself providentially *called* at this time to set apart," etc.; "and, therefore, under protection of Almighty God, I have this day set apart," etc.

4. And hereby is precluded all irregular and uncalled-for ordinations by presbyters who have no such "exigency" to show for their act. Wesley said in 1755: "It is not clear to us that *presbyters* so circumstanced as we are may appoint or ordain others," since the providential call had not then come; nor can it be inferred from all this that our polity is properly presbyterial, for, though the fountain of the ordaining power is in the Church and presbytery, yet the presbyterial act of ordaining is extraordinary, and with design of preserving the episcopate. If all the bishops were dead, the elders would ordain new and proper bishops; and if both elders and bishops were dead, the people would rightfully ordain new ones.

"From all this it follows that, in strict churchly order, on the principle stated by Hooker, Wesley's ordination was legitimate, and no Episcopal Church has a right to reject its episcopacy. It is, in fact, an emancipation of the episcopacy from all despotic successional trammels, and the restoration of the free and voluntary episcopacy of the primitive Church.

And as our Church was organized before either the Roman or the Anglican ordinations in this country, so we were the first regular established Episcopal Church in America." (Whedon.)

Well did Arthur Edwards, D. D., say in an article on "Relations of the Methodist Episcopal Church to the Historic Episcopacy," in the *Methodist Review*, November–December, 1889, pp. 853–4: "We are persuaded that there is less ground to doubt the validity of Wesley's ordination of Coke on ecclesiastical grounds than of many and vital episcopal ordinations during the Elizabethan days of the reformation in England."

Albeit, suppose it be conceded that the right of ordination was not allowed to Mr. Wesley in the Established Church of England, it must yet be recognized that, by reason of his providential relation to the Methodist societies in America his right of ordination therein was coextensive with their apostolic right to constitute a Church with a ministry in orders.

"What Mr. Wesley did in the premises he did because of his acknowledged *jurisdiction* in the Methodist societies and the exigency of the times." (Emory's "Defense of Our Fathers," p. 34.) "Mr. Wesley invested Dr. Coke with 'episcopal *authority*' only in relation to the Methodists in America. In relation to *other* Churches, Dr. Coke had no 'episcopal *authority*;' nor did

Mr. Wesley claim to give him any. In this respect his language was considerate and precise. Neither have the bishops of other Churches any 'episcopal authority' in relation to us, nor could they confer such authority among *us* on any individual without *our* act." (Ibid., p. 47.)

What Mr. Wesley did he did as a Methodist. To be sure the usual order of procedure was reversed or varied. Ordinarily the Church acts first as a body in constituting or receiving a minister, or giving its consent or issuing its order for conferring the proposed authorization, and then for the ceremony of ordination or consecration to take place. Nevertheless, "a subsequent recognition of an act of an agent, by his principal, makes the act as valid as though it had been previously directed to be done." We tend to think of Mr. Wesley and the Methodist societies as two distinct parties, when, in fact, they were not two but one. The measures of Wesley in the ordination of Dr. Coke, etc., must be reckoned as a part of the work of the organic act. The circumstances, the long distances, and the length of time then required for travel, together with Mr. Wesley's advanced age, made it impossible for him to be present at the Christmas Conference, and made it necessary for the imposition of hands to precede the formal action of the Church. But as his initial act was at their "request" (see sketch on the "Origin of the Methodist Episcopal Church," published in all editions of the Discipline), and also ratified by the formal action of the Church at the Christmas Conference, it gave it all the force of its *own* action, and as if Mr. Wesley had been personally present in the act of organization.

"The office of Mr. Wesley in the organization of the Church, and the institution of her ministerial orders, is plain. *It was simply an office of very special fitness.* It could not be more. . . . Nor was the initial part of Wesley, in any sense, necessary either to the organization of the Church or to the institution of her ministry. On his consent, or without it as well, the preachers might have assembled in conference, just as they did in Baltimore, and resolved the societies into the Methodist Episcopal Church with complete validity in the organization. Then they might have authorized the ordination of certain preachers to the order of elders at the hands of Asbury, and in turn his own ordination by these elders to the order of a bishop, with the function of further ordinations; and our orders would have been just as valid as they are with the offices of Mr. Wesley, directly on his own part and mediately through Coke, just as valid as any claimed to have proceeded from the hands of the archbishop of Canterbury or of the pope himself, and possessed of quite as much grace. And to the persistent prelatical demand for the source of our orders, let the answer be as constant—*in ourselves;* and let it be as confident as constant.

"Still, there was a very special fitness in the initial offices of Wesley. The American Methodists were his affectionate spiritual children, and, by their own repeated election, entirely subject to his authority. With these facts of relationship, and his own personal pre-eminence, it was most natural and proper that they should seek his help in the present need. Nor was there any other who might so fittingly initiate the necessary measures of relief. Even his own orders, while not necessary to a valid ordination, were yet an element of fitness in the exercise of this function. With the right of ordination in the societies, and the part of Wesley taken on their own petition, and the approval of his part openly by the people and formally by the preachers in conference assembled, the institution of our ministerial orders lacks no element of either fitness or validity." (Miley.)

It was the Church that ordained. The absence of the laity from the organizing body has been the topic of some remark. However it is not especially significant. The preachers were looked upon as their representatives, as much as if formally chosen for that purpose. They were not needed in the business of that conference; besides, their absence was with their own consent, while the conference met their desires and had their approval.

It was the Church that ordained. If this doctrine be deemed High-Church, it can be only as it respects the prerogatives of the Christian body in matters of economy; but it is assuredly and decidedly Low-Church as to the prerogatives and functions of ministerial orders.

Dr. Whedon well said: "The ordination of Coke by Wesley, which seems to be slightingly styled a 'unique affair,' has long appeared to us one of the grandest acts of Wesley's life. It cleared American Methodism at one brave stroke alike from all Presbyterian movements, all Anglican claims and internal schisms; and from that time to this, thanks be to God! we have stood out before Christendom on our own high plane, 'rejoicing as a strong man to run a race.' It seems too slightingly said, also, that 'Wesley had been appealed to by various persons' to give us a Church government. He did so after the union above described, in compliance with the unanimous request of American Methodism, patiently waiting for four years. If popular assent makes ecclesiastical government legitimate, no act was ever more legitimate, no government was ever more legitimate, than Wesley's in this matter."

No people on earth are further removed from slighting ecclesiastical order—indeed none more truly exalt it, none maintain more thoroughly the perpetuity of the Church, and have a more strict regard to regularity in all investitures with office in the Church, than Methodist Episcopal Churchmen. They would dread the disorders of an unauthorized ministry, and avoid it as carefully as the most clamorous advocates of transmissionism. They abhor schism. The truly catholic Church has no other visible organization than that which it has in its particular constituencies. If any particular Church, therefore, refuses to fraternize with other particular Churches, without Scriptural ground for the refusal, it is guilty of schism. If a particular Church exacts unscriptural terms of fraternization of other Churches, then that Church, and not the other Churches which refuse compliance, is guilty of schism. If an individual refuses to commune with a particular Church, without Scriptural ground for the refusal, he is guilty of schism. If a particular Church exacts unscriptural terms of communion of the individual, then, as before, that Church, and not the individual who refuses the compliance, is guilty of schism.

"Separation from a true organic Church is justifiable only on the grounds of the *right of revolution*. On any less ground it is schism," says our Dr. Whedon. The measure of responsibility of those who, in any period and in whatever way, have originated schism, is the magnitude of the sin involved—that of dividing and rending the Church of Christ, which is "his Body." Albeit, schism when it becomes *necessary* is not schism at all. Moreover, a person or number of persons, who never belonged, in any way, shape, or manner, to any given ecclesiastical order or organization, and therefore could not separate from it causelessly or otherwise, can not, on any principle of justice or legitimate reasoning, be liable to the charge of schism. Of one thing this people are very certain: they are not schismatics either in spirit or in fact.

Charles Wesley, the distinguished brother of the eminent John, who, in his letter to his brother on the latter's ordination of Dr. Coke to the superintendency, or episcopate, in America, avers himself a transmissionist in the words, "Whether the uninterrupted succession be a fable, as you believe, or real, as I believe," put the argument of prelatical successionism satirically thus:

> "So easily are bishops made,
>   By man's or woman's whim;
> Wesley his hands on Coke hath laid,
>   But who laid hands on him?"

The answer is, the preachers and people of the Methodist societies in America, when performing the organic act by which they became a divinely constituted organism, a body of believers in covenanted compact, providentially associated for the ends and purposes of the Christian life—a Church by the vote by which they "accepted" Mr. Wesley's act as their own.

The doctrine of derivation standing, as it does, impregnably upon the apostolic precedent and principle, we declare that *the bishop is the creature of and proceeds from the Church, and not the Church the creature of and proceeding from the bishop.*

Withal, the ordinative act of John Wesley, he being a presbyter in the Church of England, and a minister of the gospel in Christ's Church *in* England—for, though the former was and is political, the latter, through all the mutations of the centuries, was and is spiritual, their historic lines sometimes crossing each other, but seldom coinciding for any considerable period—together with the friendly assistance of Rev. Philip William Otterbein, a presbyter in the German Church (subsequently founder of the United Brethren in Christ), in setting apart Francis Asbury to the bishopric, are pivotal points in the processes by which the Methodist Episcopal was evolved from the general historic Church without the figment of transmissionism.

Section III.

HARMONY OF METHODIST EPISCOPAL STRUCTURE WITH NEW TESTAMENT USES OF THE WORD CHURCH.

1. The local Church entity is maintained, its autonomy preserved, its interests subserved, its power magnified. The gifts of the Holy Spirit, so freely and variously distributed among the people, must be utilized for the attainment of Christian character and the development of a New Testament Church. Life is more than law. If there be not life and power in the members of the body, the body itself will be dead. In addition to the hearing of the word and attendance upon the ordinances, there must be proper attention given to the admission to the flock of those who may be deemed worthy, and the exclusion therefrom of those who are shown to be unworthy; the genesis of a proper officiary for the local Church, and delegates or representatives in the interests of the general body; and the management of matters of temporal economy, current expenditures, pastoral support, and the propagation of the gospel in all the earth, as provided for in all these things in the New Testament constitution of Christ's Church. Such are the things that are done by these local Churches, themselves of the general Church, or their properly constituted representatives, the leaders and stewards' meeting, or the official board and the quarterly conference.

2. The Federative, or Connectional Church, is a marked characteristic of this organism. A compact and visible oneness, a solidarity, an entire union or consolidation of interests and responsibilities, is secured. Avoiding the rigors of absolutism on the one hand, and the excessive leniencies of pure democracy on the other, it is truly ecumenical, its membership in all parts of the earth constituting its entirety, welded together in connectional bonds. Thus is the broadest view of the field, which is the world, presented, harmonious action is given to all the parts, and executive effectiveness secured through connectional officers, and the annual and other conferences.

3. The Church representative finds no truer exhibit anywhere than in the quadrennial delegated General Conference, exercising its New Testament prerogative as a Christian council in such legislative enactments as the demands of the work, from time to time, require.

Thus has the Methodist Episcopal Church been guided by the hand of Providence to its present status. It has been well said, "Governments are not made, they grow;" and equally well said, "Things that grow are better than things that are made." May the same kindly and powerful Hand guide this organism in all its future growth!

Section IV.

MINISTRY—ORDERS, OFFICES, PREROGATIVES.

In conformity with the New Testament pattern, this Church consists of laity and ministry; the latter consisting of those who have been "moved by the Holy Ghost" thereto, as evidenced by "gifts, grace, and usefulness." While some religionists have held that the ministry of religion to the world is supplied with laborers from time to time, by the voluntary offerings of men, as men choose a profession or enter upon an occupation in the secular affairs of life, Methodists have held that the supply is by the direct, personal appointment of the Savior himself—the Head of the Church; this is his "call." And they have and do still set more store by, and have been and are still ready to yield more honor to, the evidences of "a divine call to the ministry," together with the proper authorization by elective and ordinative methods, "by the authority of the Church," than to any possible setting apart without it—"though hands of bishops, archbishops, and popes may have been imposed sufficient in number to thatch a cathedral." The divine call is the basis of a valid ministry. God has the first vote. On such a basis this Church provides in her book of Discipline, "that no person shall be licensed to preach without the recommendation of the society of which he is a member, or of the leaders and stewards' meeting." Thus the initial point of approbating and accrediting a preacher is with the Christian body, it recognizing the suitableness of the candidate; and from this point onward, this Church holds within itself, by its regularly constituted methods, the power to advance the candidate, step by step, to final, full investiture, with full ministerial eligibility and authority, and to refuse so to do, if that be her judgment. Thus every man who has gone forth to preach, with the authorization of this Church, has been chosen thereto, after the apostolic pattern, from the common priesthood—the body of believers. It is the Church that elects; it is the Church that ordains,—"By the authority of the Church" (see Ritual). An eminent Methodist Churchman, Daniel Curry, D. D., said: "Whatever of authority abides in the ministry is not a foreign importation, but the outgrowth of the Church's vitality, and by the power of the Holy Ghost." Another, D. D. Whedon, D. D., said: "It is the call of the Church to test and judge of the 'call' of the minister. It is not sufficient for a man to start up and declare, upon his own motion, that he is 'called,' to authorize him to exercise the organic ordinances of the

Church. It is in the Church that lies the duty and right to furnish, from her own bosom and hand, and to authenticate and externally commission the ministry. Herein lies 'the priesthood of the people,' that out of a holy people shall go forth a holy ministry."

To those assigned to the order of ministry, this Church gives the New Testament titles of order and office, namely: Deacon, *diakonos;* elder or presbyter, *presbuteros;* and bishop, *episkopos,* from *episkopeo,* to look upon, to inspect or watch over. The analogy of the word bishop—Saxon, *biscop*—to the second and third syllables of the word *episcopos* is obvious. By a reference to the status and duties of each, as set forth in the Discipline, it will be seen that, while an elder or presbyter is a minister who, without further explanation, is fully ordained to and invested with the sacred office after the New Testament pattern, the deacon[*] is but partially invested with ministry, he being an apprentice and servitor. The bishop is an elder, or presbyter, to whom has been added the function of a general superintendency or overseership.

---

[*] The temporal concerns of the Church have been placed in the keeping of the laical office of steward, which office conforms in spirit and purpose with the work of the "seven" (Acts vi, 2-7), who are commonly called deacons in some other Churches; but Dean Alford says: "The title of deacons is nowhere applied to these seven in Scripture, nor does the word occur in Acts at all" (*in loco*).

Thus, having the office, he very properly and fittingly is given the official designation of the office, the title of bishop; not the same, however, in signification as that of a stilted ecclesiasticism, which surrounds it with adventitious dignities, as in the prelatical episcopacy of the papal and Protestant High-Church hierarchies, and to which John Wesley so stoutly objected, and very properly, when viewed from that stand-point, but the plain and unpretentious bishop of moderate episcopacy, just such as a New Testament Church may indicate, in harmony with that of the primitive Church.

As to the question raised with great frequency, whether the term "order" may be applied to the bishopric, as indicating a class or grade of ministers distinct *from* and superior *to* the elders of the Church, there is an ambiguity in which the true meaning can be determined only and entirely by the particular meaning attached to the term itself when used: "If the term be understood as describing such an order in the ministry as established by the express authority of God, and as essential to the existence of a Christian Church and a valid administration of the ordinances, then Methodist episcopacy is not held, in the judgment of our Church, to represent a third order in the ministry. The Methodist Episcopal Church not only admits, but asserts and maintains, and has always so done, by her highest and her humblest authorities and by all the grades between, that in this sense bishops and elders are inherently and essentially the same order in the ministry. Its episcopacy was originally and avowedly instituted on this principle, and still rests on this doctrine. In 1844 the bishops of our Church, all of whom have long since laid their well-worn armor by, in their address to the General Conference, said: 'With our great founder, we are convinced that bishops and presbyters are the same order in the Christian ministry, and this has been the sentiment of the Wesleyan Methodists from the beginning.' To the soundness of this doctrine I may here say, and not with bated breath, that the present bishops of the Methodist Episcopal Church give a most hearty and unanimous consent.

"At the same time it must also be equally held as the doctrine of our Church that this original and essential equality does not render it unlawful for elders, in circumstances which to them appear to make it expedient, to delegate to one of their own order a more extensive power of oversight, or to commit to some one or more of them, as organs of the body, a larger executive part of that power which originally and fundamentally was common to them all. And this is the real source and spring of the power and authority of Methodist Episcopacy, so that our episcopacy is derived, dependent, and responsible. Its authority is a delegated authority only, and may be modified just as the body of the eldership, from which it was derived, shall see proper, and that, too, without any infringement on the rights of the bishops themselves.

"Now, by just so far as this delegated authority gives to the bishops a more extensive oversight and a wider sweep of executive duties, by just so far, and no farther, may they be considered a third order in the ministry of our Church. In other words, the bishops of the Methodist Episcopal Church are an order of ministers distinct from and superior to other elders of the Church in that extent of jurisdiction, and in those executive duties delegated to them by the body of elders, and in no other respect. Such is Methodist Episcopacy as to the source of its authority, and as to the sense in which it is one order in our ministry distinct *from* and superior *to* the eldership of the Church." (Bishop W. L. Harris, in "The Relation of the Episcopacy to the General Conference," pp. 38–40.)

The writer distinctly remembers that in the military service, in each camp or post, there was each day an officer detailed, called "the officer of the day," who had a supervisory care of all things throughout the camp or post, and who while he held that position was, in respect to his particular line of duties, virtually in command, being in that much the superior of his equals and even of his superiors in rank. Nevertheless, he was, after all, only an officer of some certain grade or rank, as a lieutenant or a captain. Thus the bishop, as such, is in an office, and not in an order higher than the eldership—a presbyter, plus the power of oversight, and for prudential reasons with a life-long tenure of office. "There never had been anything in the history of the Church, in its legislation, its rubrics or ritual, that hinted, even by remotest intimation, that the elections and ordinations to the episcopacy were any less permanent than were the elections and ordinations to the eldership; and it would be now just as inconsistent with the law and usages of the Church, and no less incongruous with her entire history, to deny a life-tenure to her episcopacy as to deny a life-tenure to her eldership." (Harris, "Relation," etc., p. 46.)

However, the whole matter is subject to the mandate of the Church, through her constitutional methods; for, as Professor Miley says, "Orders are degrees or grades in the divinely instituted ministry, and are severally determined by the measure of invested functions. This measure is not divinely ordered, and could not be without the fixation of a complete Church economy which must not yield to the slightest variation. Much, in fact, is left to the freedom of the Church in matters of polity. In these true and accepted views it clearly appears that orders arise from functions, not functions from orders. The Church, in her freedom, determines the orders by the distribution of sacred offices."

Viewed through the spectacles of some denominational rivals, not to say adversaries, a Methodist bishop is a despot without a rival this side the Vatican, beheld in the light of disciplinary duties and restrictions; namely, to preside in the conferences, but without voice or vote or privilege of debate; to travel through the connection at large, overseeing the spiritual and temporal business of the Church; to ordain such as are elected to orders by the conferences, but no others; to change, receive, and suspend preachers in the interval of the conference sessions, governed in changing and receiving by the necessity of the case, and suspending only as the "Discipline may require"—that is, after due examination and conviction before a committee of the peers of the accused; to decide all questions of law that may arise in an annual conference, the application of the decision being with the conference, and from such decision any aggrieved may appeal to the Judicial Conference; to fix the appointments of the preachers, and such, too, only as the Church, by her own act, may furnish for appointment,—he becomes a simple preacher of the gospel, burdened with fearful responsibilities and onerous duties, and in their discharge hedged about by the necessities of the work and that regard for the rights of others which must come to every right-minded man, impelled by the mightiest moral motives that can move a human being freighted with ponderous responsibilities for God's cause, and prompted, withal, by the very instinct of self-preservation; for the Church gave him the stationing power, and if that power be abused she may take it away and lodge it elsewhere; hence he can not play the tyrant to any appreciable extent without feeling the sharp ax of ecclesiastical deposition on his episcopal neck.

Seeking for principles, leaving polemics to contend over names, we note striking conformity to apostolic models: "And God hath set some in the Church first apostles, secondarily prophets, thirdly teachers, . . . helps, . . . governments." (1 Cor. xii, 28.) Whether Timothy and Titus were fixed bishops or were evangelists, at least two things are logically inferred: First, that the superiority of some Church officers over others, in jurisdiction if not in orders, is not contrary to Scripture precedent; second, that it was not repugnant to the constitution of the Churches of the apostolic times for men to have the power of jurisdiction over at least more than one particular congregation or Church. (See Emory's Defense, etc.) Titus performed his allotted duties in Crete. (Titus i, 5.) Homer (Odyssey, Book XIX), in speaking of Crete, says:

"Crete awes the circling wave, a fruitful soil,
And ninety cities crown the sea-born isle."

Do not Methodist bishops travel in large districts, or portions of country, containing cities like that of classic song, ordaining men whom the Church has designated for the work of the ministry, and "setting in order the things that are wanting," generally? Did not the prophets teach? Do not Methodist traveling and local ministers teach the people in the elements of the Christian faith? Did not the "helps" designated discharge co-ordinate duties in the local Churches? Do not exhorters, stewards, and class-leaders discharge similar duties in our Churches? The analogies are striking; our practices are apostolic.

Notwithstanding the high prerogatives of Methodist bishops, from Coke and Asbury to the end of the list, there has never been one who has dishonored the Church, nor for whom she has had occasion to blush; but by their fidelity, industry, wisdom, courage, and piety, in the administration of the vast and ever-growing interests of the Church, they have not only called forth admiration for the genius of her institution, but have demonstrated hers to be a real apostolic episcopacy. Errors of administration there doubtless have been, for infallibility is not claimed, as for the popedom by its adherents; nevertheless, such sagacity, disinterestedness, and success have been unequaled in all churchmanship.

As seen by the duties incumbent upon the Methodist ministry, its *prerogatives* have always been understood to be simply ministry as heretofore defined, and never priesthood. Its commission has been understood to be not simply "go, conduct service," or "read prayers," or "administer the ordinances," but "go, preach." Thus the command of Christ, and thus Paul, when he counted it his highest honor and joy to be a preacher of the gospel: "Unto me, who am less than the least of all saints, is this grace given, that I should preach among the Gentiles the unsearchable riches of Christ." Again, very far from believing the doctrine of baptismal regeneration, in the first Epistle to the Corinthians he thanks God that he had baptized none of them but Crispus and Gaius and the household of Stephanas, and then adds: "For Christ sent me not to baptize, but to preach the gospel." Thus, too, the preaching of the Methodist pulpit has aimed to be a full, clear, and explicit enunciation of the way of the sinner's approach to God; of the nature of saving grace, and the mode of its attainment; of the operations of the Holy Spirit; of the attainability of evangelical perfection of character; of setting forth Christ in his offices of Prophet, Priest, and King; of promulgating the doctrines of the Christian faith and the ethics of the Christian life.

In doing this, there have been certain broad, *philosophical* principles which have characterized and given force and efficiency to these ministrations, namely:

(1.) Consciousness as a law of belief and a source of knowledge.

(2.) The reliability of human testimony, under the safeguards and restrictions of the laws of evidence, as a law of belief and source of knowledge.

(3.) Assurance of the favor of God as a deep want, a crying need, an urgent demand of the human soul.

(4.) Man's high probational advantage as a free moral agent.

These, with a theodicy or theory of the divine government over moral intelligences, based on that high, noble, rational conception of the character of Deity expressed by St. John, the divine—namely, "God is love"—together with the ever-deepening conviction that to the moral nature, the heart, and life, every Biblical truth should be directed, has given to this ministry a truly apostolic power.

Section V.

COMBINATION OF QUALITIES OF VARIOUS FORMS.

The advocates of the popular or democratic element in Church government delight to quote in its advocacy such Scriptures as Matt. xxiii, 8–10: "Be ye not called rabbi, for one is your Master, even Christ; and all ye are brethren. And call no man your father upon the earth, for one is your Father which is in heaven. Neither be ye called masters, for one is your Master, even Christ." Also in Matt. xx, 25–27, it is said: "But Jesus called them unto him, and said, Ye know that the princes of the Gentiles exercise dominion over them, and they that are great exercise authority upon them. But it shall not be so among you; but whosoever will be great among you, let him be your minister; and whosoever will be chief among you, let him be your servant." These passages, it is contended, "recognize the essential equality of Christians under the rule of Christ; their subjection to him alone as their Lord and Master, and to God alone as their Father; and entirely exclude any spiritual lordship of the apostles, or any one of them, over the Church." If by "spiritual lordship" is meant supervision or control in spiritual affairs, then they are virtually a denial of all government administered in any way by human beings, and each one is responsible directly and only to Christ.

On the other hand, the advocates of what they call "strong government," contend that administrative functions inhere by divine law in the ministers of the Church exclusively, and can see in the New Testament only such texts as: "Feed the flock of God which is among you, taking the oversight thereof." (1 Pet. v, 2.) "Take heed therefore unto yourselves, and to all the flock over which the Holy Ghost hath made you overseers, to feed the Church of God, which he hath purchased with his own blood." (Acts xx, 28.) "The apostles and elders came together for to consider of this matter." (Acts xv, 6.)

Between these two extremes there is "a golden mean," a middle ground, which blends into beautiful harmony all Scriptures, and saves all from a party spirit. Let extremes be avoided. The Scripture truth lies between.

Strenuous advocates for the popular element in ecclesiastical government object to Methodist Episcopal order, because it does not conform in all things to that of the State. But where is there one word of Scripture requiring such a thing? If there be no command, where is the obligation? If it must conform in this country, is it requisite that it conform to the State in other lands? Is it necessary to conform to the form of political governments unless the objects to be attained are identically the same? Certainly not. The various forms of government—whether monarchical, aristocratic, republican, democratic—should be applied according to the objective point, the end to be attained. In families, primary schools, the military, the government of ships, steamers, exploring expeditions, and the like, the monarchical in form of government obtains, though not necessarily so in spirit; in some of them, in their best development, it is an elective monarchy. Large schools, colleges and universities, banks, railroad corporations, and associations of all kinds for the promotion of enterprise and improvements, are quite uniformly aristocratic in form of government, being directed by a privileged or restricted class, such as faculties, boards of trustees, or directors, etc. The democratic form finds its practical workings in incidental voluntary associations which may not be of too great magnitude for this method. The fullest political realization of this form was Athens, in Greece. In our own America, every man, who is worthy of being in it, favors in the Constitution, and in statutory enactments under it, a just balance of the republican and democratic principles.* Blind adher-

---

*These words are used in their primary and not in their partisan sense.

ence to one particular form, in all cases, would disrupt society, and violate all settled and good principles. It is folly to suppose that there is anything intrinsically wrong or oppressive in monarchy or aristocracy as forms of government. To be sure, all must be opposed to the abuse of the different forms in their application to different things. Hence, we are uncompromisingly opposed to monarchy or aristocracy in the State; to republicanism or democracy in the family, primary school, or the army; to monarchy in a railroad company, a bank, or a university, because unsuitable and unadapted to the end to be attained. Liberty or freedom does not always consist in voting or not voting on all the questions that may touch us in life, but in a firm and steady securement to us of our rights, whatever they may be, in the particular thing with which we may be identified. The objective point of Church work and life is to secure the conversion of mankind, and the procurement of the best advantages for the inculcation of religious doctrines and ethics, the administration of the holy sacraments, the development of Christian character, the promotion of the ripest piety, and the spread everywhere of Scriptural holiness. From the standpoint of Biblical teaching and the necessity of the case must the form of ecclesiastical government be decided, and not from the particular form of government which may chance to obtain in the State. Such a principle would give to the Church forms varying with the diversified forms of earthly governments.

Methodist Episcopal organism is not, confessedly, a pure democracy, but is an amalgam or union of the best features of the three regular forms. As previously shown, the tendencies of power are to accumulation in the direction in which it is vested. Despotic governments grow more absolute. Democracies tend to give individual liberty at the expense of the great general good. A well-balanced constitution is mild in its *spirit* and *tendencies*. The proof of this is seen in the modifications which have taken place as circumstances indicated to be desirable. That the representative principle obtains largely is seen in the method by which her ministry is primarily constituted—approbated. As previously indicated, the laity of the Church is, at the initial procedure, in every case the responsible party. And it is a striking fact that, while particular Methodist Episcopal Churches can not select their immediate pastor, yet the pastoral office is reached only by successive steps watched over by the laity and sanctioned by their formally expressed will; yet in many sister Churches, which boast of their thorough democracy or republicanism, the ministerial candidate is approbated by some association, council, or presbytery, in which the laity bear a very subordinate part, if any; they being consulted but inconsiderably until the question arises which, of the many ministers furnished to hand, shall be their immediate pastor.

Then, too, Methodist Episcopal laity control the matter of admission to the Church; for none can be admitted who has not, like a good catechumen, proven himself or herself worthy by a six months' probational period, and then been recommended by the leaders and stewards' meeting, all laymen, and a public examination before the Church as to his faith and purpose.

Furthermore, in the law-making body of the Church, the quadrennial General Conference, the laity as well as clergy are represented by their own properly constituted delegates, the peers in voice and vote of any.

Additionally, ministers or members, accused of moral derelictions and delinquencies which would exclude from the kingdom of grace and glory, are, by the constitutional provisions of this Church, guaranteed a trial by their peers, confronted by their accusers, and even then they have an appeal to the judicial or the quarterly conference. Thus are the rights of all secured, the honor of the Church sustained, and the glory of God promoted. Methodistic Church organism is founded in a principle of true republicanism.

It is true that John Wesley said, "We are no republicans and never intend to be;" but this was said in England, with English surroundings; but this did not bind the associative action of the American Methodists when the hand of Providence called them into independent Church life.

While the advocates of a purely republican or democratic ecclesiastical government object to an *authoritative* superintendency—the bishopric and an episcopal form of Church government—they should, in order to do justly, remember that Methodist Episcopal Christians are abreast of them in objecting to any exclusive, so-called "divine right," *obligatory* form of Church jurisdiction, and to any and all prelatical assumptions of power. While their bishops are empowered with an ordaining prerogative and a superintending responsibility, and the power, within constitutional limitations, to "fix the appointments" of the preachers, yet their power and office proceed from the inherent power and the manifested will of the Church, which remains just as competent to recall that power, and withdraw its will and abolish the office, within its own prescribed limits, as it was to confer it in the beginning. Yet the principle of superintendence over ministers and Churches, and of reasonable and expedient subordination among them *for the works' sake*, was deemed not only unobjectionable, but as in some form needful, either through "boards," "alliances," "associations," "presbyteries," etc., or through a duly authorized episcopate. The latter method was chosen, not the episcopacy of monarchy, where the bishop rules exclusively, where in him inheres the right to make laws, to adjudicate and to execute; nor the episcopacy of aristocracy, where the bishop, and a privileged class surrounding him—namely, the other ministers—legislate, adjudicate, and execute; but a moderate episcopacy, the episcopacy of republicanism, where the episcopate is an office to which men are elected by those over whom they are to exercise the functions of their office,—the body of the Church, in its representative capacity composing the legislature, forming the judiciary, and appointing its executive, thus occupying conservative ground, "a golden mean" between prelacy on the one hand, and independency on the other, and balancing its legislative, judicial, and executive departments of government to a degree quite unexcelled in the great sisterhood of Churches.

Methodist Episcopal Christians, not High-Church nor Low-Church nor no-Church, but Methodist Episcopal Churchmen, approve the wisdom of the fathers in accepting a form of Church government which, on the whole, so well combines the good qualities of all governmental forms, and is so well adapted to secure unity of belief, harmony of action, and evangelizing efficiency in the vast sweep of its effort to bring the world to Christ, and accept the utterance of Rev. John Wesley, A. M., when he said: "I believe that the episcopal form of Church government is Scriptural and apostolical—I mean *well-agreeing* with the practice and writings of the apostles; but that it is prescribed in Scripture I do not believe."

Section VI.

Some Methods.

Itinerancy, or that method of distributing ministerial workers and talents in vogue in Methodism, has well been called its "stamped feature." That the method is thoroughly *Scriptural* is seen in the fact—

(1.) That the Lord Jesus, the Head of the Church, himself set the *example*. The three years of his ministerial or official life were spent in the itinerancy; that is, in traveling and preaching; or, in the language of Peter (Acts x, 38), he "went about doing good."

(2.) His *instructions* to his apostles exhibit the itinerant plan for the propagation of the gospel as the true method. Mark xvi, 15: "Go ye into all the world and preach the gospel to every creature." Matt. x, 5–7: " These twelve Jesus sent forth, and commanded them, saying, Go . . .

to the lost sheep of the house of Israel. And as ye go, preach, saying, The kingdom of heaven is at hand." Matt. xxii, 8, 9: "Then said he to his servants, The wedding is ready, but they which were bidden were not worthy. Go ye therefore into the highways, and as many as ye shall find, bid to the marriage." Matt. xxviii, 19: "Go ye, therefore, and teach all nations." Mark vi, 7, 8: "And he called unto him the twelve, and began to send them forth by two and two; . . . and commanded them that they should take nothing for their journey, save a staff only." Luke x, 1: "After these things the Lord appointed other seventy also, and sent them two and two before his face into every city and place whither he himself would come." Luke xiv, 23: "And the lord said unto the servant, Go out into the highways and hedges, and compel them to come in, that my house may be filled." The imperative "Go!" of our divine Lord demonstrates that a *sent* ministry is the divine plan.

(3.) The disciples and apostles *obeyed the injunctions* of their Lord, and acted on the itinerant system. Matt. xxii, 10: "So those servants went out into the highways, and gathered together," etc. Acts viii, 4: "Therefore they that were scattered abroad went everywhere preaching the word." Verse 40: "But Philip was found at Azotus: and passing through he preached in all the cities, till he came to Cesarea." Acts xv, 36: "Paul said unto Barnabas, Let us go again and visit our brethren in every city where we have preached the word of the Lord." These quotations are ample to prove that the itinerant system is the true primitive, apostolic, New Testament plan of operation in the Church of God.

Moreover, itinerancy is expedient because (1.) It is always safest and best to follow the primitive Scriptural and apostolical system according to the pattern in the mount. (2.) Comports in genius and spirit with the aggressive, universal and missionary design of the Christian ministry and Church in the conquest of the world. The gospel must be aggressive till it is universal. (3.) Gives a holy independence to the ministry in denouncing and warning of sin without fear of dismissal therefor. (4.) Distributes as equitably among the Churches as is possible on earth diversified ministerial talent and efficiency, and is thus comprehensive in its educational force. (5.) Is the strongest possible ligament of union between the local Churches, producing a sentiment of unity throughout the entire connection, renders the ministry the common property of the whole Church, in which every society and member has an interest, and giving to such minister a corresponding and reciprocal concern for all the societies. In a sense in which those of other systems can not say, the people of this communion can say: "All things are ours, whether Paul or Apollos or Cephas." Because of a common interest and sympathy, real Methodists can properly use the Scriptural and amiable appellation "brother." (6.) Is economic, making possible the grouping into "circuits" of Churches which could not singly and alone afford competent support, and, at the same time, accommodates in "stations" such as can. It saves waste of time in pastoral changes. (7.) Affords a continuous pastorate, the office being permanent, though the incumbents change. (8.) Affords the highest mental stimulus to pulpit preparation, and incites to immediate and earnest effort to till the allotted field. (9.) Avoids bondage to persons or local combinations, and secures the freedom of loyalty to impartial law. (10.) While characterized by a touch of the military that harmonizes with that attribute of the Church called militant, preserves the mobility of ministerial forces, preventing them from huddling where not wanted, and sends them where needed, those forces, like men in the emergencies of war, going forth in a spirit of obedience to leaders whom they themselves have chosen by constitutional representation— the measure of their obedience being of their own devising, and not prompted by base servility, but by a heroic spirit of self-sacrifice and devotion to Christ and to duty, which not only invigorates their efforts but which allies them to the Christian toilers of the apostolic age. Indeed the itinerant method, as experience has proven, profiteth much every way.

Now, when the Lord Jesus ascended upon high he constituted the Church as his body (Eph. i, 22, 23), which is, therefore, to be hands and feet, and eyes and brain, and tongue and will to do the things for him which he would do for himself were he bodily upon the earth. He *sent* the workers into the vineyard. It therefore devolves upon the Church as such to send the toilers into the field, not leaving it to individual caprice.

The itinerancy obtaining, then, the method necessitates an authorized appointing power, a responsible executive, if it be conserved and maintained in fact as well as in name. The ministers and Churches can not adjust the forces in such a system and preserve it, for that would at once become the elective and not the itinerant system; nor could committees of laymen and ministers, with local predilections, local views, and local interests, be sufficiently disinterested nor disengaged from personal and local considerations, to make equitable and successful assignments; therefore this power is vested in a legally constituted EPISCOPATE, chosen by the ministers to be appointed and the Churches to be served, through their delegated representatives, to do this very work for them; and thus is the episcopal act, in "fixing the appointments," the act of the Church—the Body of Christ—itself; the episcopal prerogative not being inherent, but vested "by the authority of the Church," which may, if it so desire, recall it and lodge it elsewhere. But where else could it be better vested than in a simple, primitive, God-honored episcopacy, occupied by men of mature years, experience, and judgment, who, with a life-tenure of office, can have no other possible motive than to perform their duties with the utmost impartiality and efficiency?

Properly enough are the incumbents of this office given the New Testament title of bishop, as shown on a previous page.

Plainly, now, the episcopacy, if it be efficient, must touch every part of the Church, and this must be done either by the incumbent personally, or through a subordinate—a sub-episcopacy—appointed as a representative responsible to itself.

In the adoption of the plan of general superintendency at the inception of the Church, the latter method was adopted, leaving the episcopacy to the general superintendency purely, and constituting the PRESIDING ELDERSHIP. "There never has been an episcopal Church, of any great extent, which has not had *ruling* or presiding elders, either expressly by name—as in the apostolic Churches—or otherwise, *in effect*. On this account it is that all the modern episcopal Churches have had their presiding or ruling elders under the names of grand vicars, archdeacons, rural deans, etc. The Moravians have presiding elders, who are invested with very considerable authority, though, we believe, they are simply termed elders. And we beg leave to repeat that, we are confident we could, if need were, show that all episcopal Churches, ancient and modern, of any great extent, have had an order or set of ministers corresponding, more or less, to our presiding or ruling elder, all of whom were, more or less, invested with the superintendence of other ministers." (Notes on Discipline, 1796.)

Objections to this office usually come either from those who have not examined into the important relations thereof to the whole economy of the Church and its necessitated place in an episcopal system, or from those who have a bias against an episcopal form of government; unhappily, too, sometimes asserted, notwithstanding a sacred covenant that they " will cheerfully be governed by the rules and regulations of the Methodist Episcopal Church." Methodist *Episcopal*,—not Methodist *Independent*, nor Methodist *Congregational*, nor Methodist *Presbyterial*, but Methodist *Episcopal!* The office is representative of the unity, the solidarity, of this covenanted compact—the link of connectionalism between the local Churches; it is a combination of official functions, the incumbent being a traveling evangelist, preaching not by sufferance, but authoritatively; his first Disciplinary duty being to "travel," *i. e.*, perform the duties of a traveling preacher in his district; then to exercise official oversight in his allotted jurisdiction; and thus is prepared to serve as an auxiliary to the episcopacy in making the annual assignments to posts of pastoral labor; and so making operative the itinerant method, with its many advantages, and preserving the equilibrium of the Church. The efforts of non-episcopal Methodism to operate an itinerant system, without the episcopal and sub-episcopal offices, have met with very indifferent and fragmentary success. Abolish the office of presiding elder, and in order to preserve our general itinerant plan and to render the episcopate available, it will be necessary to have about as many bishops as we now have presiding elders, which could not be either more economical, if as much so, nor as efficient as the present method. Let modifications occur as exigencies demand, but let the office be preserved; for no other function of the system, not excepting the episcopacy itself, is capable of greater usefulness, or that could not be sacrificed with less peril than this; the episcopacy could not proceed without it, while it might possibly, even though clumsily, operate the system without the episcopacy. To fail to sustain, in all legitimate ways, this, one of the most economical and efficient executive arms of service in this system, is revolutionary.

That method of pastoral oversight called the *Class-meeting*, is another striking characteristic. That large class of Scripture texts which bespeak not ministerial, but mutual, care among Christians (Heb. x, 24, 25; Acts ii, 42; Rom. xiv, 19; xv, 14; 1 Cor. xii, 25; Gal. vi, 2; Eph. iv, 16; Col. iii, 16; 1 Thess. v, 11; James v, 16), contain within them, in some part or *in toto*, the charter of this exercise, which affords the most desirable opportunity for self-examination as to whether overcoming the love, cares, and maxims of the world, we are working out our salvation, is conducive of regular religious habits, ministers to Christian union, and promotes "the communion of saints."

One writer on the constitution of the primitive Church sums thus: "The result of my investigation is as follows: First, when the number of Christian believers was sufficiently large in any locality to form a society or congregation, their theory of organization was substantially like that of an ordinary prayer-meeting, such as is held by devout laymen among us at the present day; or, second, when a body of converts to Christianity had been made by the preaching of an apostle, it would seem that he, ordinarily at least, selected certain persons to watch over them, and to instruct them essentially in a manner analogous to what is done by the *class-leaders* in the society of Methodists. In an ensuing age, after the decease of the apostles, the members of these several associations or congregations, however originally formed, henceforth selected their leaders by some formal expression of their own approbation." (McCulloh.)

Love-feasts, fellowship-meetings, feasts of charity, patterned after the *agapæ* observed in the Apostolic Age,* came into Methodism by the way of Mr. Wesley's observations among the Moravians,—simplified, so that, in the symbolism of good-will toward each other in Christ Jesus, no rich or costly viands appear to the possible perversion of wicked men; but a bit of common bread and a sip of water, with no sacramental signification whatever, bespeak the fact and practice of Christian fellowship. Accompanied with brief voluntary statements of experience in the things of God, commingled with songs of joyous praise, they consummate the *twofold* purpose of the institution, and constitute, as has been well

---

*Neander's "History of Religion," Vol. I, p. 325. Waddington's "Church History," p. 46.

said, a festival worth more than all the saints' days that can be put into the calendar.

The *Modes of Worship* chosen are primitive and simple, and yet sufficiently elaborate to raise the congregation to the highest pitch of devotion. Dr. Schaff says (History of the Christian Church, Vol. I, pp. 456, 461–5): "The several parts of the primitive public worship were patterned, not after the gorgeous temple service, but after the greater simplicity of the synagogue." Therefore, leaving those who have "a taste" for an "attractive service" of written formulas, to lavish their praises of "excellent," "admirable," "perfectly beautiful," or "incomparable," upon their "all but inspired liturgy," the Methodist Christian worships with Bible and Hymnal as the only prayer-book (except for the sake of uniformity in administering the ordinances) and breviary. And while Churches of sacerdotal character or tendencies leave open some door to their edifice, that the faithful may, singly and alone, worship in their way, this Church, in common with the evangelical Churches of Christendom quite invariably, sustains the mid-week prayer service, or prayer-meeting, where, in a social capacity as worshipers, its people may spend the devotional hour, and, by sacred song, and reading Holy Word, and Spirit-prompted prayer, and mutual exhortation, be lifted into a spiritually susceptible state, and so worship God in spirit and in truth, and thus be comforted and strengthened in that consecrated time, the sweet hour of prayer.

In social and public devotional exercises, in maxim and practice, *free audible responses** obtain among Methodists, thus avoiding the spiritless punctilios of liturgical responses, on the one hand, and the dead level of repression of all responsiveness on the other. For the practice

---

* This has furnished possibilities for occasional outbursts called shouting, which can not be other than rightful when the honest expression of the heart is stated. Albeit, demonstration has never been considered synonymous with the spirit of adoption, nor loud crying as a sure criterion of true repentance; and while the emotions are considered to be as holy as the intellections, yet no merit has been attached to great feeling, and the more certainly none to manifestations of emotion. These incidental expressions of joy have unhappily sometimes been exalted by weak persons into regular institutions, and made tests of the genuineness and the exaltedness of piety. To steer clear of such evils without checking the spirit of a true Christian zeal, and producing a reactionary coldness, has been the aim of the intelligent and thoughtful in this communion.

"We love a piety blending holy emotion with intellect. We know the rich power of spiritual joy. We thank God for the religion which has, in all ages, made men weep and shout, and has even resulted, through human infirmity, in jerks and catalepsies; but we desire no effort to promote the weeping, shouting, jerking, and catalepsy as a distinct institution. We love in our home the gladness and buoyancy which make our children noisy and riotous, but it is no disparagement to our parental love that when the *noise* and the riot become special

there is much Scripture precedent. The singing of psalms and hymns and spiritual songs (Eph. v, 19,) occupies an important place in devotional exercises, no other collection, assuredly, surpassing in poetic beauty and sacred sentiment our psalmody and hymnology, entering, as it does, into the details of experience, touching the heart with tenderest pathos, describing the first emotions of penitence and the highest rapture of sa-

---

objects, or assume indecorous forms, we take measures to abate the domestic nuisance; and specially when the noise is cherished by them as in itself a source of pleasure, arousing the nerves by its concussions and exciting the animal by its negation of restraint, it is an act and a duty of parental kindness not only to suppress the demonstration, but to correct the taste that enjoys it. With just the same view as a pastor, we love in the Church the rich devotion which prompts to earnest manifestation; but, as we think, nature itself teaches that such manifestation is rather to be an irrepressible accident than an object; that it is never to be made an aim; that when unchecked it is very liable to assume unseemly forms and extravagant lengths, and that its encouragement is very apt to produce a sensuous love of the nervous excitement and to engender a very unintelligent style of piety. . .
He who wishes to cultivate extravagant religious demonstration in itself as an object simply, cherishes a forced and false enthusiasm; and when, in addition to that, he rebukes as false professors the Christians who maintain a chaste reserve, he becomes censorious and condemnable. He then exhibits the 'enthusiasm with an infusion of the malign emotions,'—which is, as near as we can recollect, Isaac Taylor's exquisite definition of fanaticism." (Dr. Whedon, in *Methodist Quarterly Review*, October, 1859, pp. 666, 667.)

cred joy, by which the soul is given a part in the heavenly harmonies of the saints, and all the experiences that lie between as well, and, at the same time, presenting to the understanding one of the finest bodies of sacred theology extant.

It is the inherent right, assuredly, of every ecclesiastical as well as civil body to indicate in its compact, or constitution, the conditions of membership—how citizenship in it may be attained—and that the applicant has no right to dictate nor to complain on account of such regulations or conditions, his coming being voluntary and his admission a sufferance. This Christian body has, from the beginning, maintained its system of definite, fixed *probationary membership*. Membership in God's Church is an instituted means of grace. The method by which any Christian body admits applicants to its associative compact is wholly prudential. Is there not Scriptural authority, warrant, and precedent for examining professed converts previous to admitting them to Church standing? May not the Church, then, take what time it may deem sufficient for the examination and preparation therefor? And in taking considerable time, there is the indorsement of the primitive Church. There have been catechumens in some form in the Church from that era. Every Christian body, in its own way, applies these facts and principles.

What is so cheerfully appropriated by each ought to be just as cheerfully conceded to all.

Two classes of persons are admitted to probationary membership by this Church: First, baptized children, enrolled in children's classes; second, seekers, or inquirers, and converts. The method is in harmony with the evangelistic or revival-meeting mode of work which so much obtains among us. Some other method might be more suitable with other ways of working; as, e. g., waiting punctiliously for accessions only from well-known persons and families in the parish; but with the present modes of work we can neither bring converts into membership hastily and abruptly, nor yet suggest, even constructively, that they are probably deceived and would better keep out indefinitely, or possibly permanently. The former endangers the purity and reputation of the Christian body; the latter leaves the professed convert to the wiles of the adversary. By the system of probationary membership both extremes are avoided. The privileges of the Church, as they relate to growth in grace and in a knowledge of our Lord and Savior Jesus Christ, are afforded, both services and sacraments. The only privileges withheld from the probationer are: First, his name may be dropped at any time, without a trial by a jury of his peers, if, after a fair opportunity has been given to prove his or her sincerity and earnestness, and they have failed to do so—none being dropped, however, as long as they seem to be earnestly endeavoring to live a life of godliness. If, on his or her part, the probationer becomes weary of the company the Church affords, or its requirements, he may have the relation discontinued without asking the *consent* of the Church. This adjustment of relations being mutual, its severance by either party is not even a constructive reflection upon either, else it were no trial. Second, the probationer is not eligible to office-bearing; *i. e.*, he can not hold any office in the Church which he would not be entitled to hold if he had not thus connected himself with the Church. But the moment full membership is consummated the relation is changed, and the person becomes subject to all the rules and regulations then existing, or which may thereafter be constitutionally formed; and there is not only the privilege of office-bearing, but the duty of performing for Christ and his Church whatever of official duty may come as the indication of Providence through the Church.

Much is said against the method, usually by denominational rivals, for partisan ends. For example: "It is keeping the convert in a corner for six months, to see if he or she will live or belong to the elect;" whereas the facts are, they have been put in special training for the largest and most robust life, and their *election* being made sure in the moment of their acceptance of the Lord Jesus Christ as a personal Savior. Let every friend of the method beware of all such speciousness, and every probationary member remember that they are traveling along a most honored way, the terminal of which many thousands of earth's best have found to be at the altar of the Church and within the blessed bonds of its covenant compact.

Section VII.

DUTY OF ALL CHRISTIANS TO SUSTAIN ECCLESIASTICAL ORDER.

It is the plain duty of all men to sustain civil order; for God has ordained that order, if not in form yet in fact, and enjoins our obedience. (Rom. xiii, 1, 7; 1 Peter ii, 13, 14; Titus iii, 1.) Our personal safety and the welfare of the world depend upon it. It becomes, therefore, a crime of no ordinary magnitude to do any thing which leads to popular commotion, to disturb the public peace, and shake or unsettle the foundations of civil society. It is not only an insult to the Almighty One by breaking his commands, but it is an injury to man by sundering the bonds which bind society together.

It is none the less plainly the duty of all

Christians to sustain ecclesiastical order. God himself has *instituted* Church polity, not in definite and prescribed form, but the thing. He enjoins subordination to ecclesiastical government as essential to the prosperity of the Church. 1 Thess. v, 12, 13: "And we beseech you, brethren, to know them which labor among you, and are over you in the Lord, and admonish you; and to esteem them very highly in love for their work's sake." 1 Tim. v, 17: "Let the elders that rule well be counted worthy of double honor, especially they who labor in the word and doctrine." Heb. xiii, 7: "Remember them which have the rule over you." Verse 17: "Obey them that have the rule over you, and submit yourselves; for they watch for your souls as they that must give account." These Scriptures are binding on all Christians, and can not be violated with impunity; and they show the wide distinction between the claims of the voluntary associations of men and those of the Church of the living God.

The Church should have (1.) A place in our petitions at a throne of grace. Since we have the privilege of prayer we should exercise it on behalf of the Church. "Pray for the peace of Jerusalem." (2.) Our hearty and energetic personal service. (3.) Our most cordial affection. She has given us a share in her large-hearted affection; therefore, with nothing less than our love and devotion can we requite her. Christ loved her and gave himself for her; and "out of Zion, the perfection of beauty, God hath shined." He who boasts of what labors he has wrought, and what sacrifices he has endured for the Church, is much as the one who boasts of what great things he has done for the mother who bore him. "If I forget thee, O Jerusalem, let my right hand forget her cunning and my tongue cleave to the roof of my mouth." Such love bespeaks jealous care for her good name and faithful attendance upon her services. (4.) Our generous contributions for her support, in order to maintain her in a state of vigor and efficiency. Since she ministers to us spiritual blessings, we can do no less than sustain her with contributions from our temporal things. Besides, this is God's plainly written law.

May the good Lord save his Church from disturbers and disorganizers—those whose disaffection has sprung from the loss of their first love, or who, like Diotrephes, love to have the preeminence and are determined to rule; or who, in a spirit of insubordination, are unwilling to be restrained by the wholesome regulations of law and order in God's Church; or who are prompted by a spirit of novelty, or have become infidel; or who, more than likely, seek to evade performing their legitimate and Scriptural part in bearing the burdens, so called, of the Church, have become malcontents, innovators, and anarchists, the worst breeds of disturbers that ever cursed State or Church; who, by their ungodly deeds, lower the standard of Christianity, produce schism in the Church, and destroy all confidence and all progress. Young reader, be faithful to your Church covenant.

Section VIII.

CONCLUSION.

The Methodist Episcopal Church conforms to, is in agreement with, indeed is, an apostolic organism. It possesses all the attributes of Churchhood—holy, catholic, and apostolic. Its sanctity or holiness, like that of the individual believer, is a holiness of relation, of privilege, of obligation, of initial and progressive realization, and of promised perfection on the condition of faithfulness, watchfulness, and earnestness; a sanctity that is real, and yet, in common with all the visible Church, held in a relative sense, the real and the relative to coincide in the time of harvest, when the tares and the wheat shall be separated. Its catholicity is apparent in its spirit, in both theory and practice, recognizing the unity of God's Church amid diversity of external manifestations, knowing that a mere external, apparent unity of profession and name, a oneness of temporary discipline and symbolism without a coordinate, entire, intellectual unity, which is impossible among unequal minds, delighting to express itself through that form, would be an intolerable burden—a catholicity which cheerfully recognizes the rights of all others in the non-essentials in which it claims liberty for itself, and which comprehends in its constitution all that is valuable in all forms of polity, thus adapting it to be a truly ecumenical Church.

Its apostolicity is manifest by its conformity, as a living organism, to the precedents, and its harmony with the principles of the Churches of the apostolic and primitive era; by its doctrines, faith, and spirit—the doctrines of Christ and the apostles, the faith of the primitive Christians, and the spirit of Pentecost—with methods and materials of work, selected from the armory of the apostolic Churches, practical and yet philosophical, and well adapted to carry the gospel to the remotest bounds of the globe; a Church which has not been at all absorbed in questions of fantastic ceremony or ecclesiastical regalia, and in which, under God, revivals have constituted its invigorating and natural festivals; which welcomes the spirit of true revival—a new life developed in the soul-saving work—a reinvigoration of the Christian spirit, love, conscience, humility, and readiness for sacrifice; abroad upon its mission, not only in centers of population, but in the veriest nooks of rural districts as well, infinitely rather than the most magnificent pageant that ever issued from the gates of St. Peter's; which would rather hear one newly converted soul say, "Bless the Lord, O my soul!" than to listen to the grandest music of the deep-toned organ that ever rolled among the magnificent arches or swept along the long-drawn aisles of the Cathedral of Canterbury.

When, at the end of time, the history of the Church of our choice and love shall be reviewed—her trials and successes, her conflicts and victories, recounted; the fields of her labor scanned, and her achievements, under God, by zealous effort to help save a world smitten with a curse, chronicled; and the vast "sacramental host," saved by her instrumentality, noted—she will stand out before the eyes of all mankind like some bright, particular star on the brow of night.

Would to God that the young generation of Methodist Episcopal Christians, to whom is committed the future of this Church, may understand their "high calling," and "acquit themselves like men!" Let them be admonished that theirs will be positions of responsibility that might well fill angels' hearts and hands, but that, if faithfully sustained on their part, will be gloriously honored and rewarded by Him who hath promised.

Well may both the veterans and the newer adherents of this faith lustily sing of this Zion, as of the Church of God in general:

> "For her my tears shall fall,
>   For her my prayers ascend;
> To her my cares and toils be given,
>   Till toils and cares shall end.
>
> Beyond my highest joy
>   I prize her heavenly ways,
> Her sweet communion, solemn vows,
>   Her hymns of love and praise."

O, ye sons of Levi, who minister at these holy altars—divinely called, properly qualified, duly constituted, and regularly appointed, preaching the doctrines the apostles inculcated, imitating their zeal, emulating their devoted virtues—yours is a glorious, unimpeachable, imperishable, unbroken, evangelical, and therefore apostolical, succession of truth and grace, through the royal line of Simpson and Asbury, Coke and Wesley, the Reformers and Church Fathers, Paul and Peter, James and John, on back and up to our Eternal Melchizedek, "having neither beginning of days nor end of life!"

> "The Savior, when to heaven he rose,
>   In splendid triumph o'er his foes,
> Scattered his gifts on men below;
> And still his royal bounties flow.

Hence sprang the *apostles*' honored name,
Sacred beyond heroic fame;
In humbler forms, before our eyes,
Pastors and teachers hence arise.

From Christ they all their gifts derive,
And, fed by Christ, their graces live;
While, guarded by his mighty hand,
'Midst all the rage of hell they stand.

So shall the bright succession run
Through all the courses of the sun:
While unborn Churches, by their care,
Shall rise and flourish, large and fair."
—Doddridge.

For this apostolic ministry we pray, in the words of Charles Wesley:

"Make good their apostolic boast,
　Their high commission let them prove;
Be temples of the Holy Ghost,
　And filled with faith and hope and love."

LIST OF AUTHORS CONSULTED.

Mosheim's Church History.
Schaff's History of the Christian Church, Vols. I and II.
The Ancient Church: Its History, Doctrines, Worship, and Constitution. W. D. Killen, D. D.
Kurtz's Church History.
The Culdee Church. T. V. Moore, D. D.
Gregory's Church History—Ruter's Edition.
D'Aubigné's History of the Reformation.
Waddington's Church History.
Apostolical Succession. Rev. Thomas Powell.
Apostolical Succession in the Church of England. Arthur W Haddan, B. D.
Apostolical Succession. Rev. A. P Percival, B. C. L.
Primitive Church. Chapin.
Vox Ecclesiæ.
Neander's History of Religion.
Lectures on Church Government. L. Woods, D. D.
Trials of a Mind in Its Progress to Catholicism. L. Silliman Ives, LL. D.
Romanism of Low-Churchism, and End of Prelacy. Rev. R. C. Shimeall.
Ministerial Commission. Windsor.
Macaulay's Essays.
Stillingfleet's Irenicum.
Genius and Mission of the Protestant Episcopal Church. Rev. Calvin Colton, LL. D.
Sermons to Presbyterians of All Sects; Supplementary to Sermons Upon the Ministry, Worship, and Doctrines of the Protestant Episcopal Church. G. T. Chapman, D. D.

The Dudleian Lecture on the Validity of Non-Episcopal Ordination. Geo. P. Fisher, D. D., LL. D.
Petrine Claims. R. F. Littledale, D. D., D. C. L.
Ecclesiastical Polity of the New Testament. G. A. Jacobs, D. D.
Church Polity. A. Stevens, D. D., LL. D.
History of the Methodist Episcopal Church. Id.
Ecclesiastical Polity: Its Forms and Philosophy. Rev. A. N. Fillmore.
Methodism: Origin, Economy, etc. J. Dixon, D. D.
Prelatical Successionism. T. O. Summers, D. D.
The Ecclesiastical Polity of Methodism Defended. F. Hodgson, D. D.
Ecclesiastical Constitution. Rev. R. Abbey.
High-Churchman Disarmed. W P Harrison, D. D.
Analysis of Principles of Church Government. M. M. Henkle, D. D.
Hand-book of Scriptural Church Principles. Benjamin Gregory, D. D.
Systematic Theologies of Watson, Pope, Raymond.
Sundry Commentaries.
Publications of the Methodist Book Concern bearing on topics discussed.

Apostolic Organism.

— BY —

J. C. MAGEE, D. D.

INTRODUCTION BY J. C. W. COXE, D. D., Ph. D.

TESTIMONIALS.

REV. DR. J. W. MENDENHALL, Editor of the *Methodist Review*, says: "Having carefully examined a manuscript entitled, 'Apostolic Organism,' by the Rev. J. C. Magee, I take pleasure in testifying to its value, both as an historical document and as a discussion of a disputed ecclesiastical problem. The author has thoroughly informed himself on the subject, and, as he writes in a style both transparent and euphonious, the paper, if published, will be enjoyable as well as profitable to those who read it. Its views harmonize with those of the Church to which they appertain, and also with the New Testament, which too often has been perverted in advocacy of an exclusive form of Church government. The publication of this manuscript will relieve the subject of some difficulties, and clear the minds of its readers of all questions as to the constitutionality and religious integrity of the Methodist Episcopal Church."

REV. DR. J. C. W. COXE says: "It is written in an attractive style: the argument is conducted in a candid and judicious spirit; the historical data adduced are ample and valid: and the conclusions reached abundantly vindicate the Apostolicity of our Church organization, without making the baseless claim of exclusive tactual succession on the one hand, or conceding on the other the futility of any attempt to identify the Church of to-day with that of the Apostolic period."

REV. A. M. MAY A. B. (Beloit College), B. D. (Union Theological Seminary), formerly Rector in the Protestant Episcopal Church, for some years past a Local Elder in the Methodist Episcopal Church, says: 'I can not claim to be especially well versed in Methodist works on the particular and closely allied line of thought, but to the extent of my knowledge it excels any thing of the kind. Excellent in conception of plan: admirably worked out; very completely covering the ground. As an argument it seems to me complete—conclusive. Historically, it is correct as far as I could find time to verify quotations from authors cited: containing enough to make the points clear and well-established, and yet not overburdened. The style is admirable."

www.ingramcontent.com/pod-product-compliance
Lightning Source LLC
Chambersburg PA
CBHW032142230426
43672CB00011B/2426